DesignOriginals

✓ W9-BZR-382

NOTEBOOK DOODLES

FabuLous FasHion

Jess ♥ VoLinski

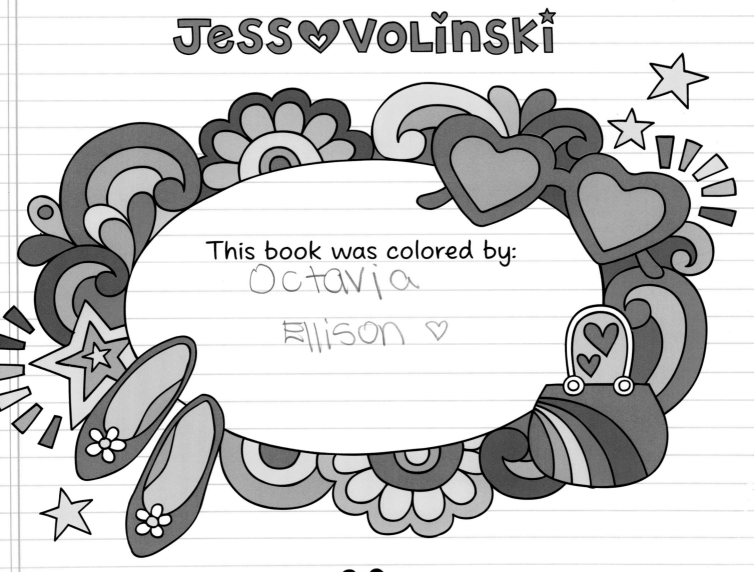

This book was colored by:

Octavia

Ellison ♡

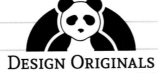

DESIGN ORIGINALS
an Imprint of Fox Chapel Publishing
www.d-originals.com

Be YOURSELF to be creative

The thing I love most about art—making it myself or enjoying others' creations—is that **art allows you to be yourself by expressing yourself.** Whatever you love, whatever is important to you, whatever makes you who you are should come out in your art. By making art that matters to you, you're starting a conversation with everyone who sees it. You're saying, "Hey! This matters to me! What do **you** think about it?"

You might be wondering, how exactly do I express myself with art? That's where **The Elements of Art** come in! You might remember these from art class. Just like writers use words to tell a story, artists use these visual elements to express themselves and start their art conversation. All visual art—whether it is a painting in a museum, storyboards for a movie, a pattern on a bag, or a coloring book page—uses some combination of these seven basic building blocks of art. Not all art has to include all seven elements, but most art will include a few.

The Elements of Art

LINE

A **line** is formed as the connected distance between two points. Lines can be thick or thin, straight or curved.

SHAPE

A **shape** is a defined area of space—a circle, square, blob, or a flower petal are all shapes.

FORM

Something has **form** if it has volume (or creates the illusion of volume). A three-dimensional sculpture has form. A two-dimensional drawing with shading that makes it appear three-dimensional can also have form.

COLOR

Color is created when light hits an object and is reflected to our eyes. A color can be described with three properties: hue (the color's name, such as "red"), value (how light or dark the color is, also called a tint or shade of the color), and intensity (how vivid or dull the color is).

VALUE

Value refers to the relationship between light areas and dark areas in a piece of art.

SPACE

Space refers to the areas in a piece of art that are around or within different parts of the art. There are two kinds of space: negative (space around areas), and positive (space within areas).

TEXTURE

Texture refers to the way the art physically feels when touched, or how an artist visually makes the art **look** like it would feel. Shading with pencils is an example of this type of visual texture.

Let's look at one of my doodles and see what Elements of Art are here. Even though this is just a simple black and white drawing, it has line, shape, and space. When you color it in, you'll probably add form, color, value, and maybe even texture. That's all seven Elements of Art—on a coloring book page! How cool is that?! Art truly is all around us!

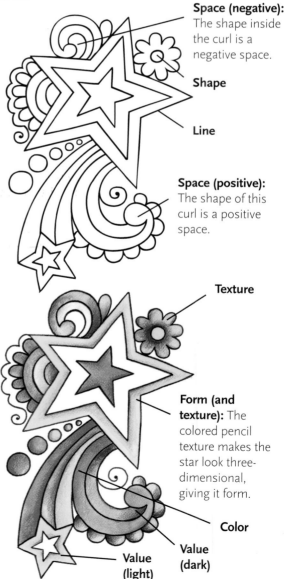

Space (negative): The shape inside the curl is a negative space.

Shape

Line

Space (positive): The shape of this curl is a positive space.

Texture

Form (and texture): The colored pencil texture makes the star look three-dimensional, giving it form.

Color

Value (dark)

Value (light)

Get inspired by COLOR

When it comes to expressing emotion, I think color is probably the most powerful Element of Art. To me, there's no better way to express how you're feeling, or how you want someone else to feel, than through the use of color. Just think of some of your favorite memories and how they make you feel. I bet color plays a big part of what you remember. Whether it's a beautiful sunset, the green of spring after a long, cold winter, or a perfectly clean, white expanse of snow, color makes a huge impact on us, both visually and emotionally. Just look at the way different colors can give the same flower drawing a completely different feel!

I've found that planning is key when working with color. If you're like me and you just **love** color, it might seem a bit overwhelming to get started. There are just so many color choices! And it's easy to fall into the rut of using the same colors over and over again, just because you like them. Making color decisions before you start can make you feel comfortable using new colors. Plus, you won't have to make a choice when you're in the midst of coloring and decide you don't like the result as much as you thought you would. A great way to try some new color combinations is to take a few minutes—it won't take long!—to create your own palettes before you get started.

Here's a fun trick I've learned for making palettes. It works especially well if you're using markers or colored pencils. Lay out all of your markers (or pencils) on a table or floor so you can see every single color you have. Pick one favorite marker (pencil) that will serve as the **anchor color** for your palette. Make it a color you really enjoy working with (or for a challenge, maybe a color you never work with!). Now, pick two or three other markers (pencils) that complement your anchor color and place those next to your anchor color to start building a palette. Keep going until you have picked five or six colors. At this point, you don't even have to use them—you're just putting them side-by-side to see how the colors look together. Keep adding or switching colors until you like what you see. It's so easy to swap different colors in and out this way. Once you have a group of colors that you like, test them out on paper to make sure you still like the way they look together. If you love it, be sure to create a sample page with the names of the markers/colors you used so you won't forget. This is a great way to quickly create a whole library of color palettes for yourself.

Another great place to get color inspiration is literally from the world around you. Color is everywhere—your clothing, your bag, even a tissue box—there are probably patterns and designs with interesting color palettes surrounding you now! I'm sure there are things you bought because you liked the colors, so use those things that you love as inspiration. I once bought a pack of hair elastics simply because they had the most beautiful combination of blues and purples. Almost anything, anywhere, can become a color inspiration, so always keep your eyes open!

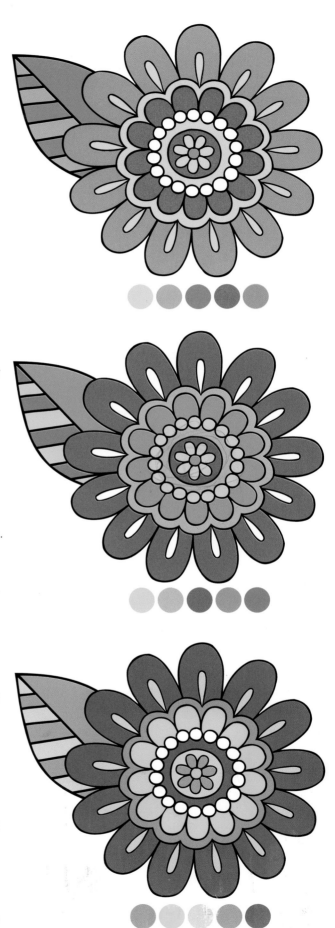

A SPECTRUM of Emotion

Color can be a great way to express yourself and define your mood. When you sit down to color, ask yourself, "How do I feel today? How can I use color to express that feeling?" Sometimes you might even feel something you can't quite put into words, but you can express it with color.

I've included some of my favorite palettes below. Each one is paired with the emotion that best describes how the color combination makes me feel. But keep in mind that everyone is different, and that's what makes art so exciting. I love to use bright colors, but maybe you like more subdued colors. My "relaxed" palette might be your "cozy." There is no right or wrong when it comes to color! Use these palettes as a starting point and see how they make you feel. Try adding or taking away a color to customize the palette to reflect your taste and style. Then, make your own page full of YOUR favorite color palettes!

The next few pages contain some colored examples. You'll see two color palettes on each page, one at the bottom and one along the outer edge. The palette at the bottom shows the design's main colors in the large circles. The small circles show lighter colors (called tints) and darker colors (called shades) of those main colors. This is to give you the feeling of this palette and visually show which colors are dominant in the design (the bigger the circle, the more dominant the color).

Along the outer edge of each page, I've included a palette with each individual color, shown separately, so you can easily match your marker, pencil, or paint colors to the colors I used.

Whether you use one of my palettes or create your own, always be sure the colors you choose reflect who you are and how you're feeling.

Now go gather up your art supplies—it's time to color!

Happy

Relaxed

Bold

Sad

Adventurous

Cozy

Wild

Silly

Romantic

Playful

Calm

Mysterious

Thoughtful

Cheerful

Serious

Dreamy

Sweet

Excited

Beachy

Quiet

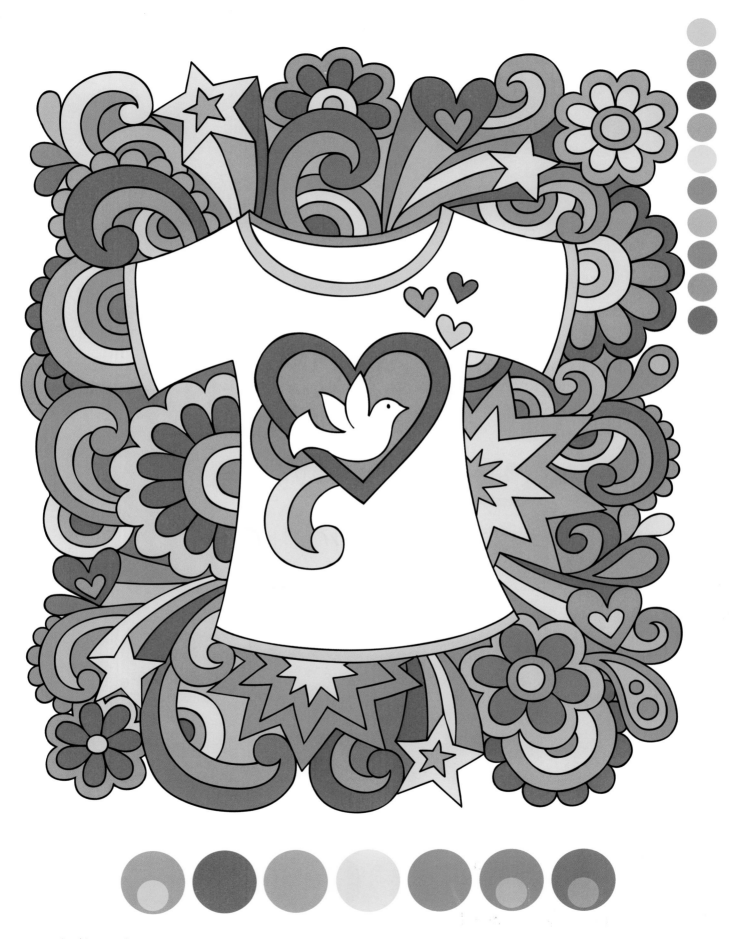

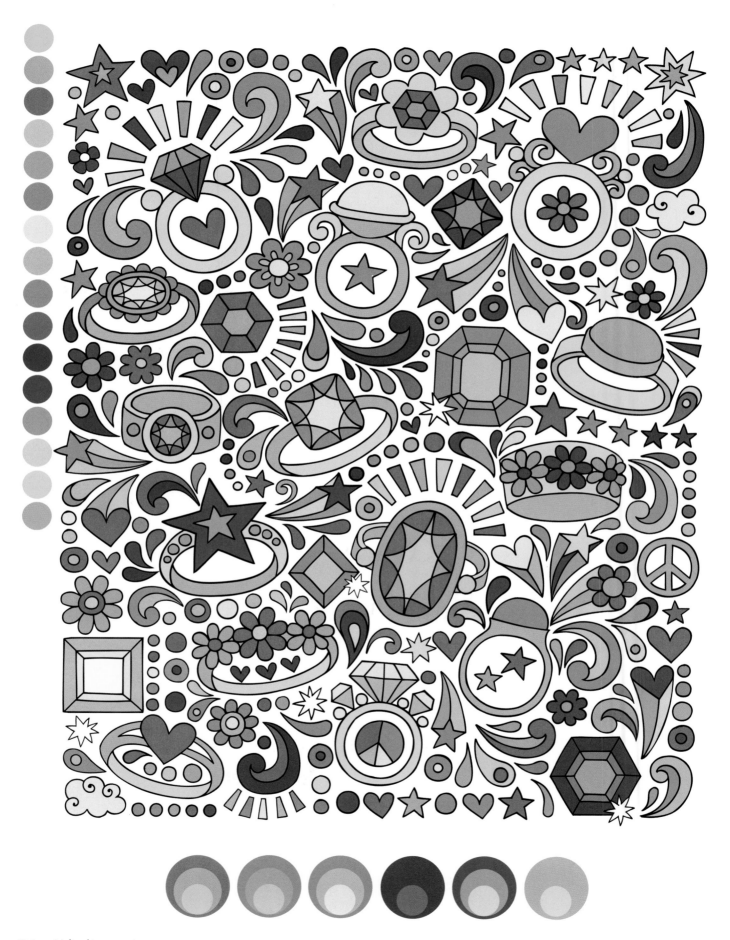

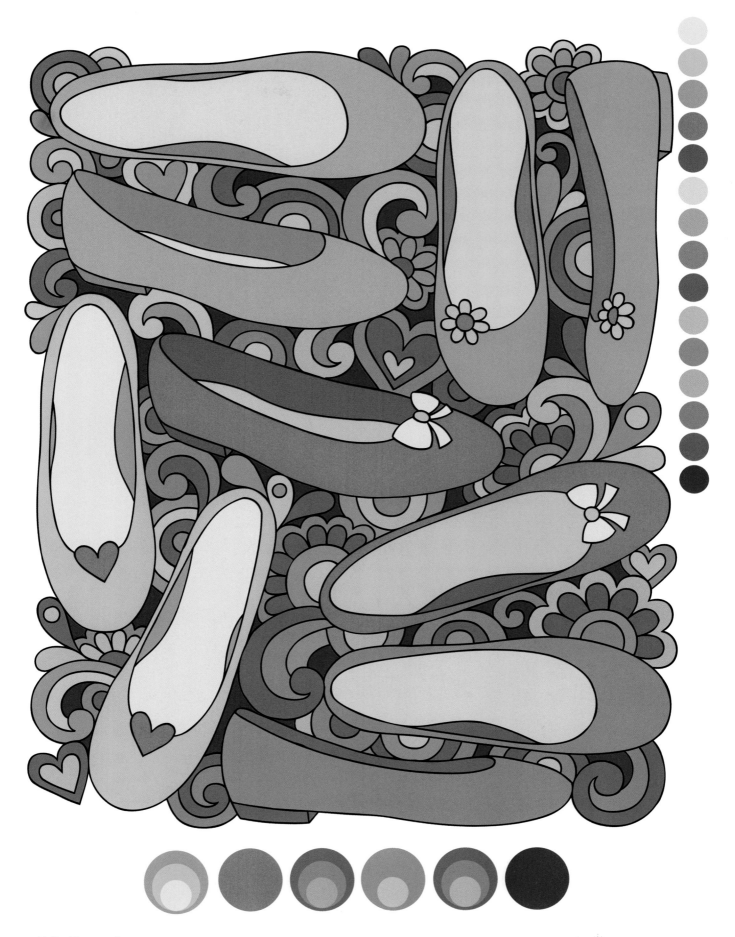

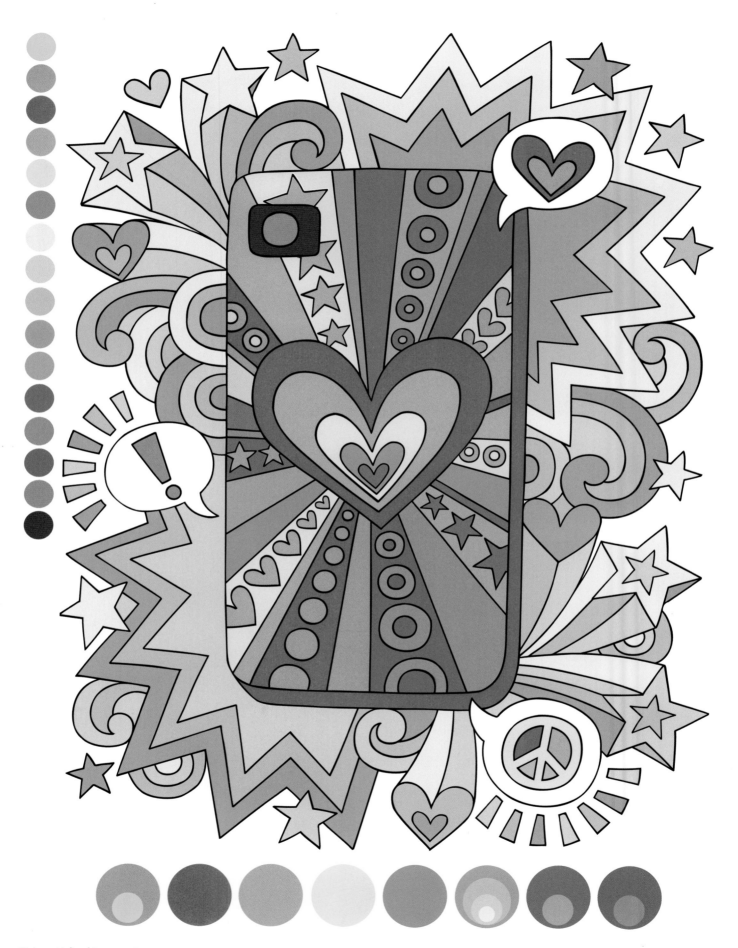

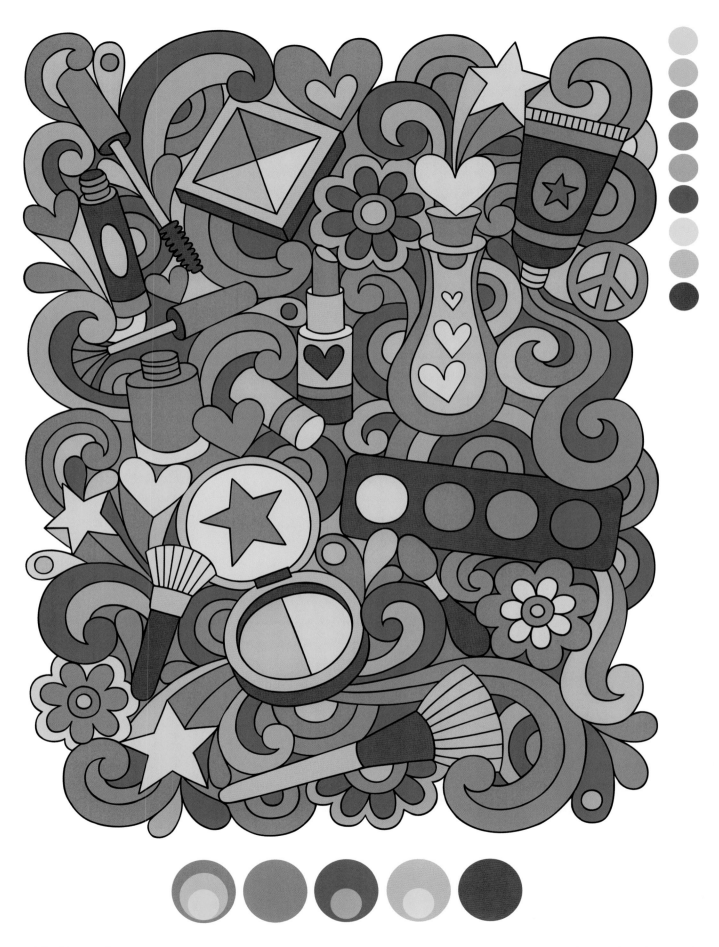

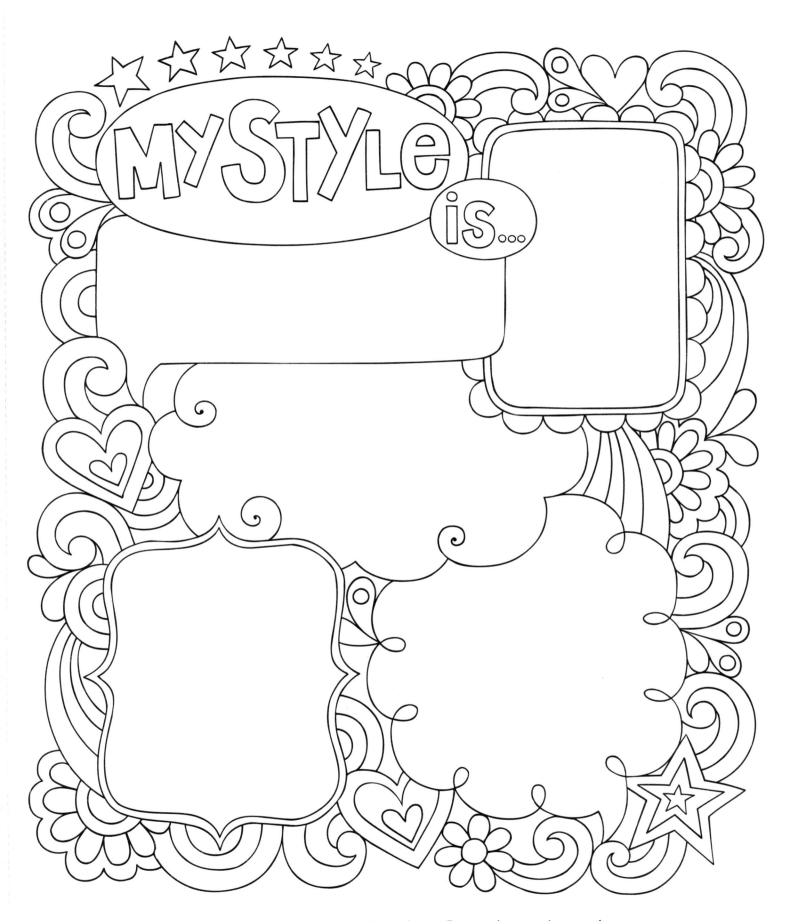

Describe your personal style in 5 words or phrases!

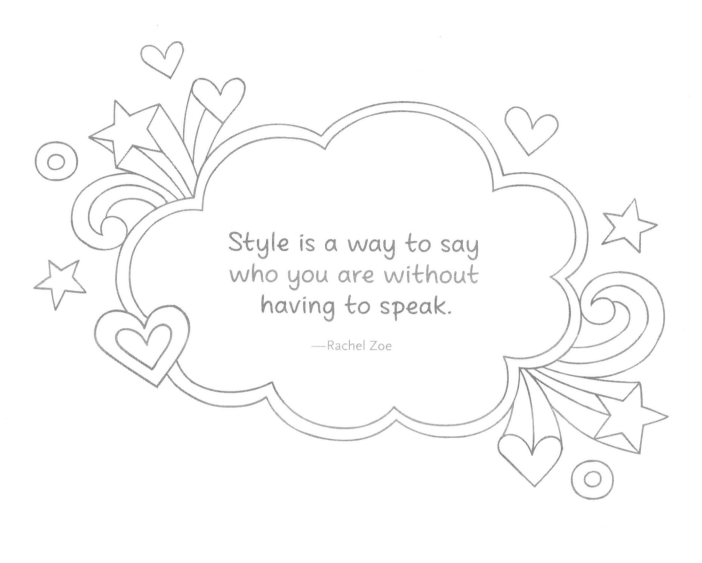

Style is a way to say who you are without having to speak.

—Rachel Zoe

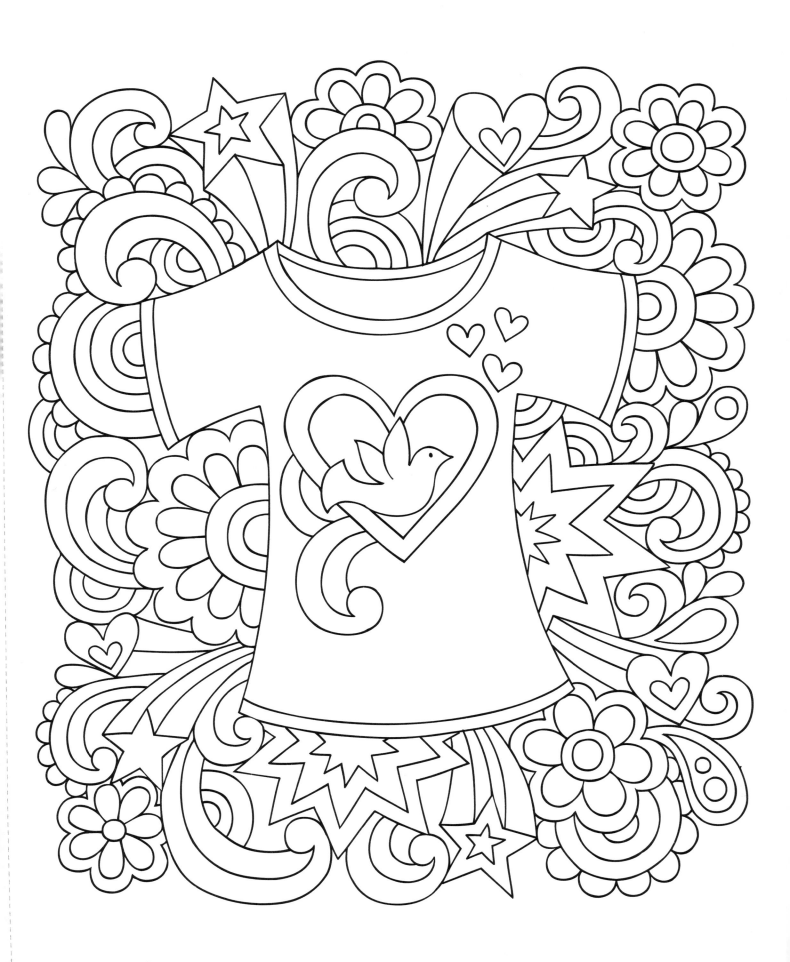

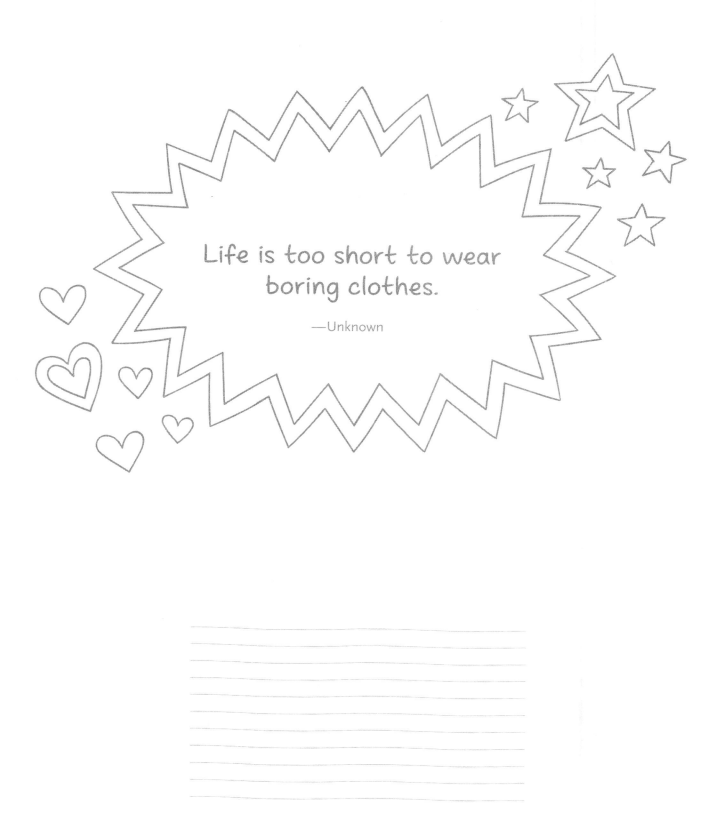

Life is too short to wear boring clothes.

—Unknown

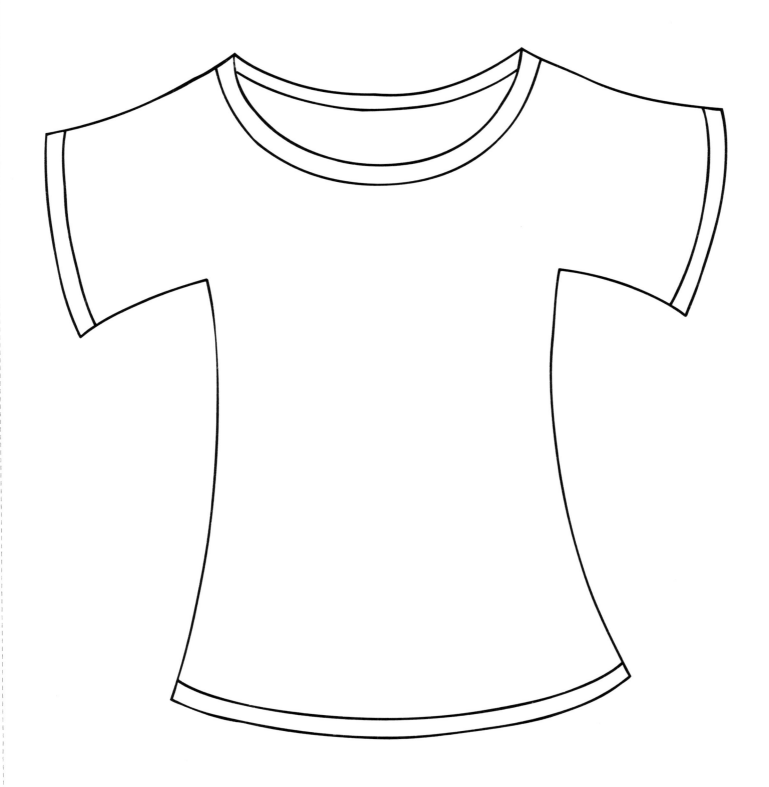

Now it's your turn! Add your own awesome graphic to the tee.

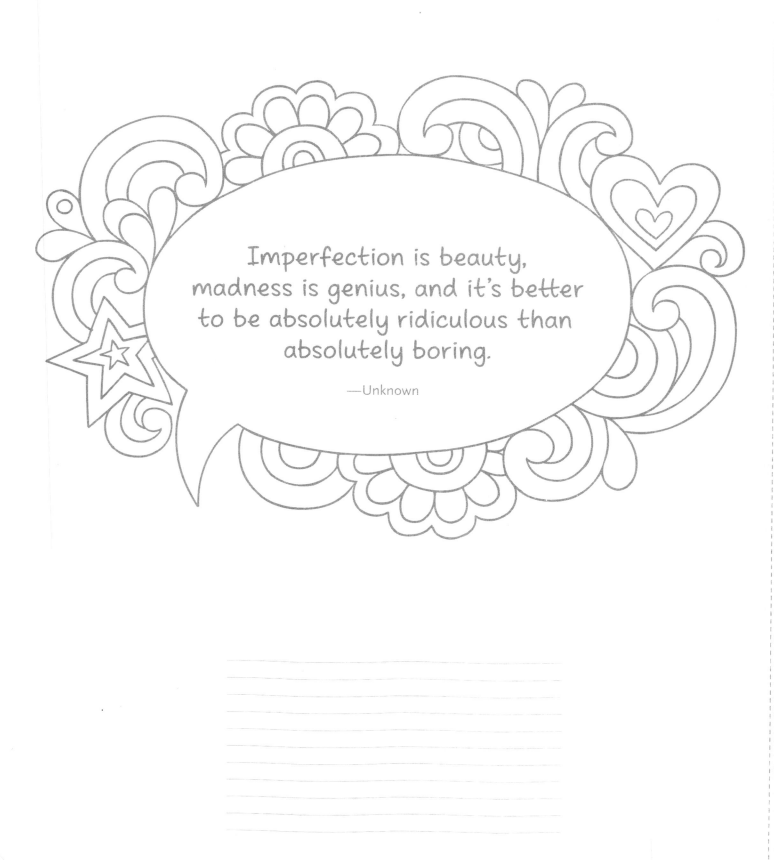

Imperfection is beauty, madness is genius, and it's better to be absolutely ridiculous than absolutely boring.

—Unknown

Decorate the patches and buttons with your own doodley designs!

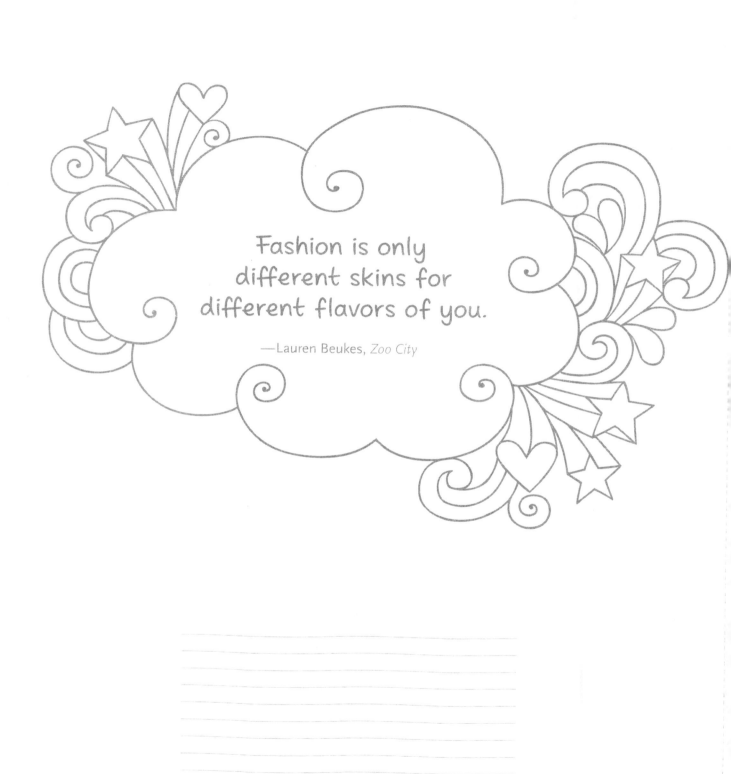

Fashion is only
different skins for
different flavors of you.

—Lauren Beukes, *Zoo City*

Decorate the sunglasses with your own patterns!

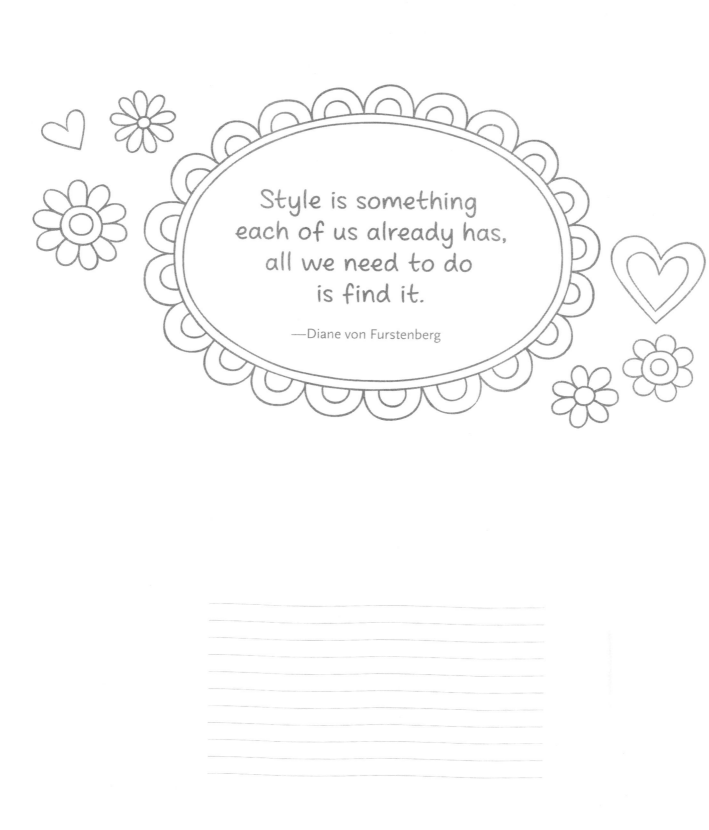

Style is something
each of us already has,
all we need to do
is find it.

—Diane von Furstenberg

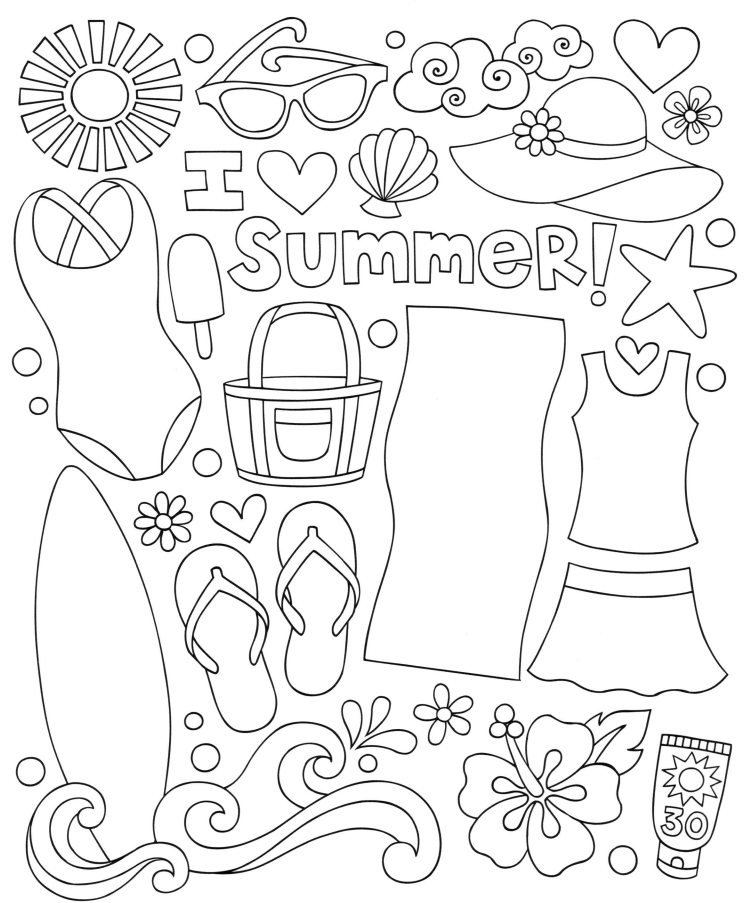

I ♥ Summer!

Fill in the open spaces with beachy patterns!

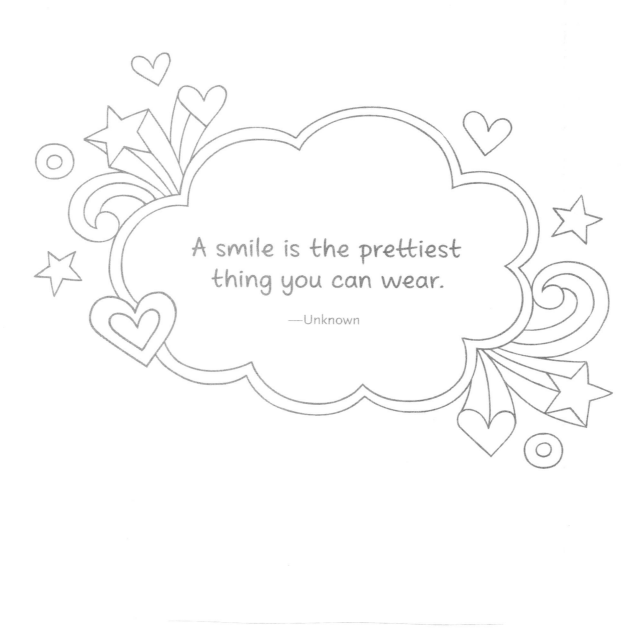

A smile is the prettiest
thing you can wear.

—Unknown

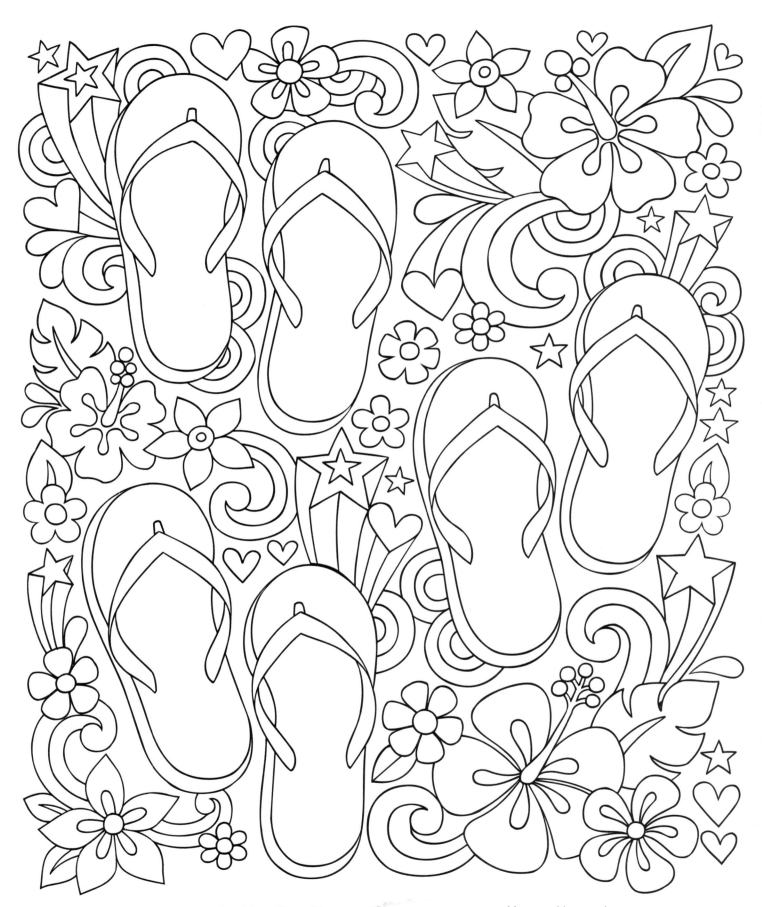

Decorate the flip-flops with your own pretty patterns!

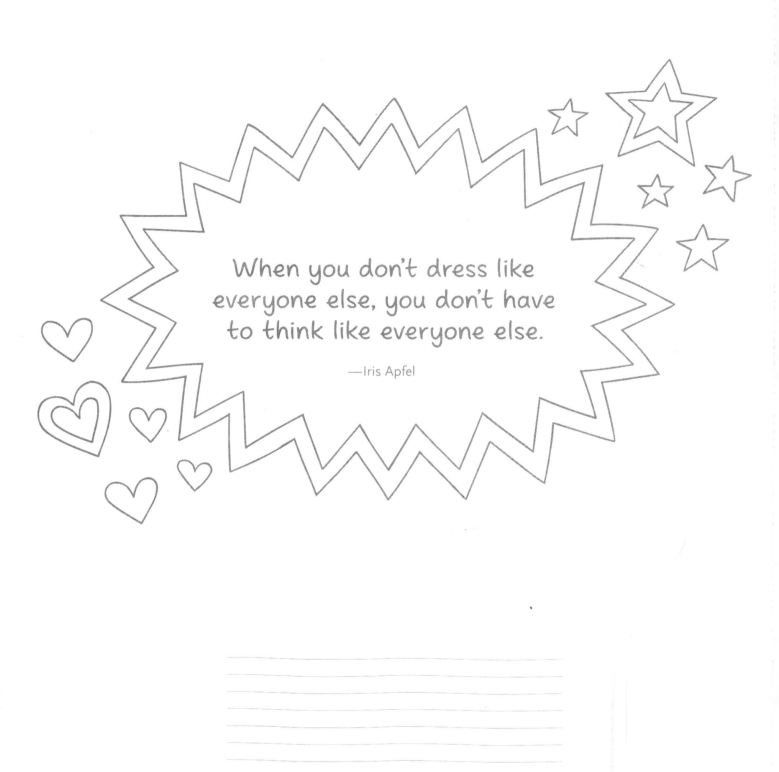

When you don't dress like everyone else, you don't have to think like everyone else.

—Iris Apfel

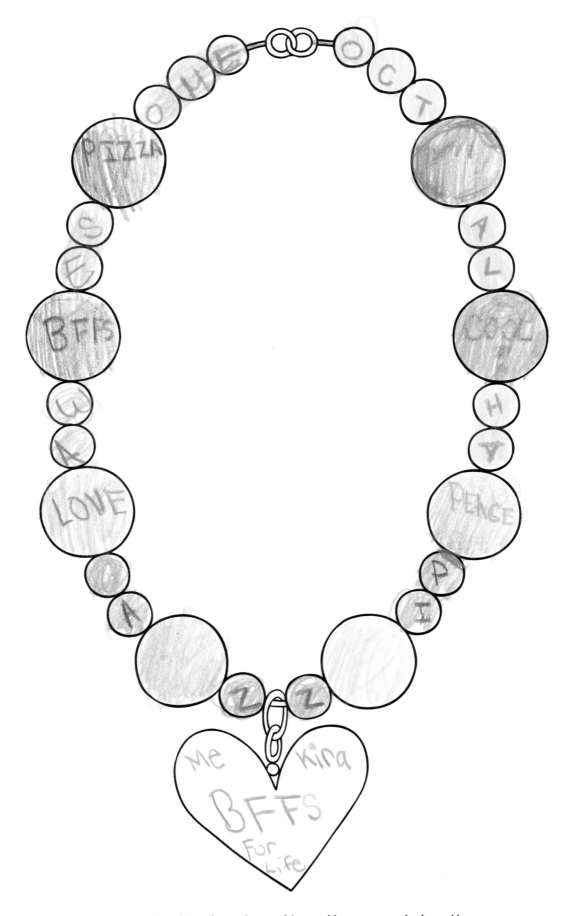

Decorate the beads with patterns and doodles.
Then add your own matching bracelet, ring, and earrings!

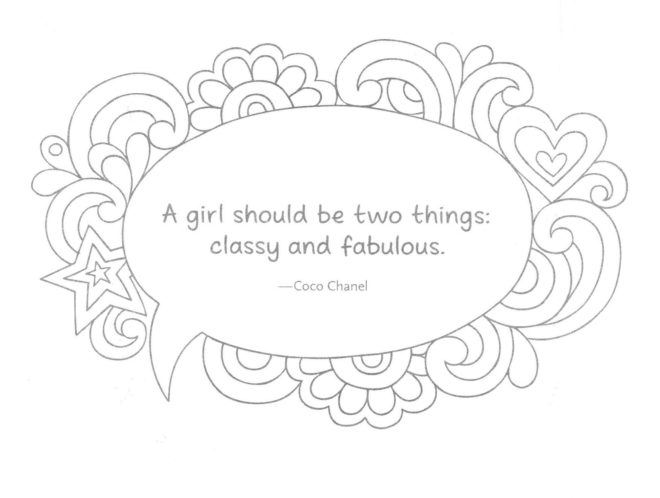

A girl should be two things:
classy and fabulous.

—Coco Chanel

_____
_____
_____
_____
_____
_____
_____
_____
_____

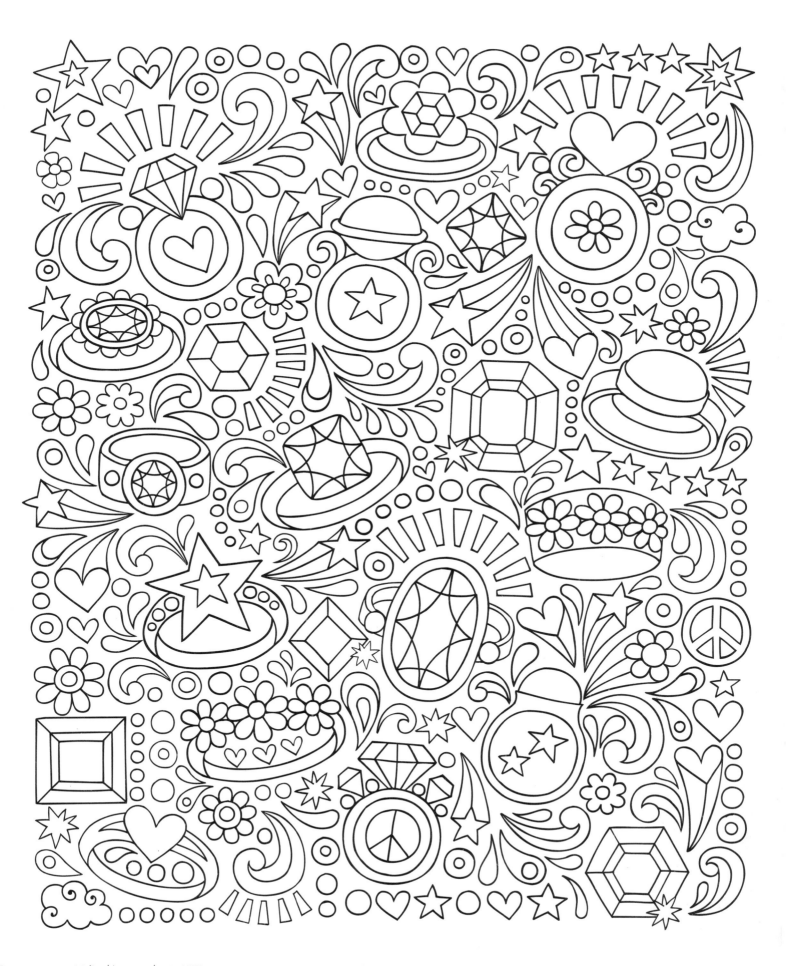

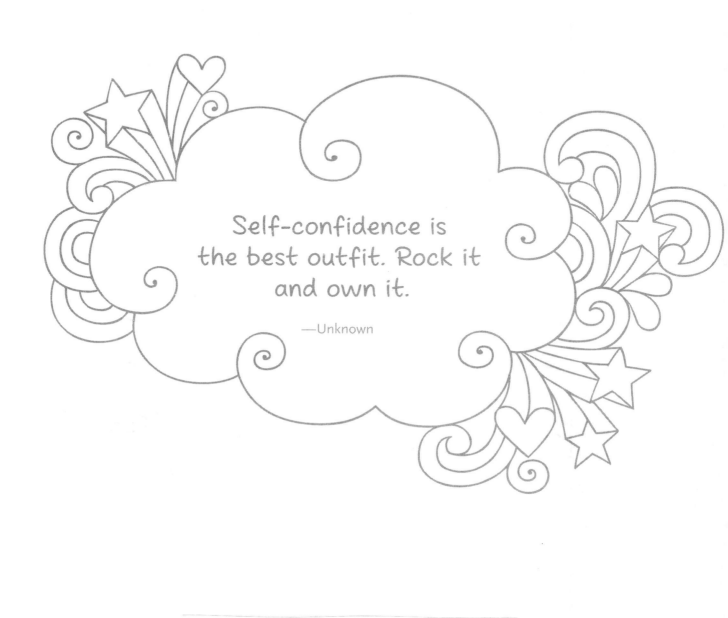

Self-confidence is the best outfit. Rock it and own it.

—Unknown

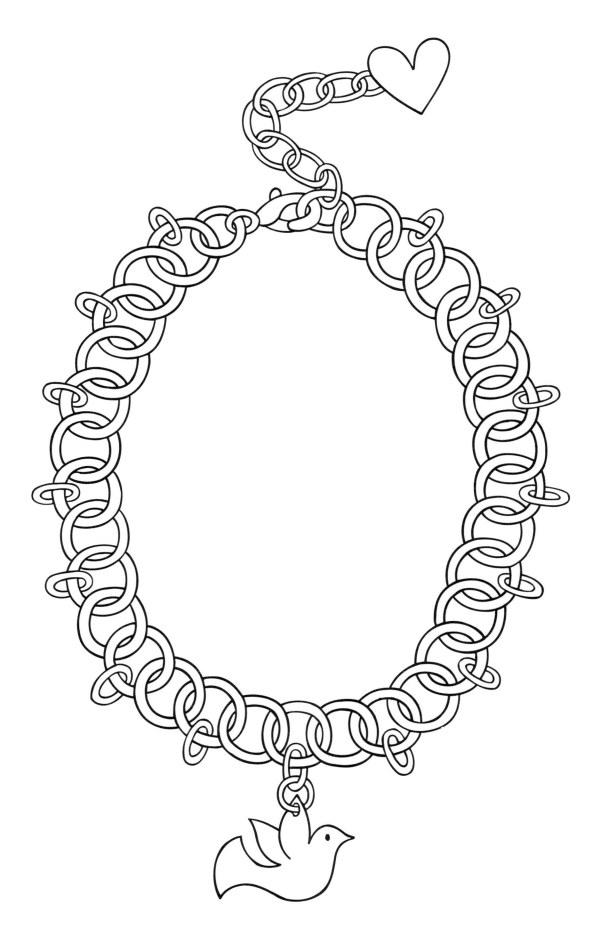

Add charms to the bracelet, each one representing something important to you!

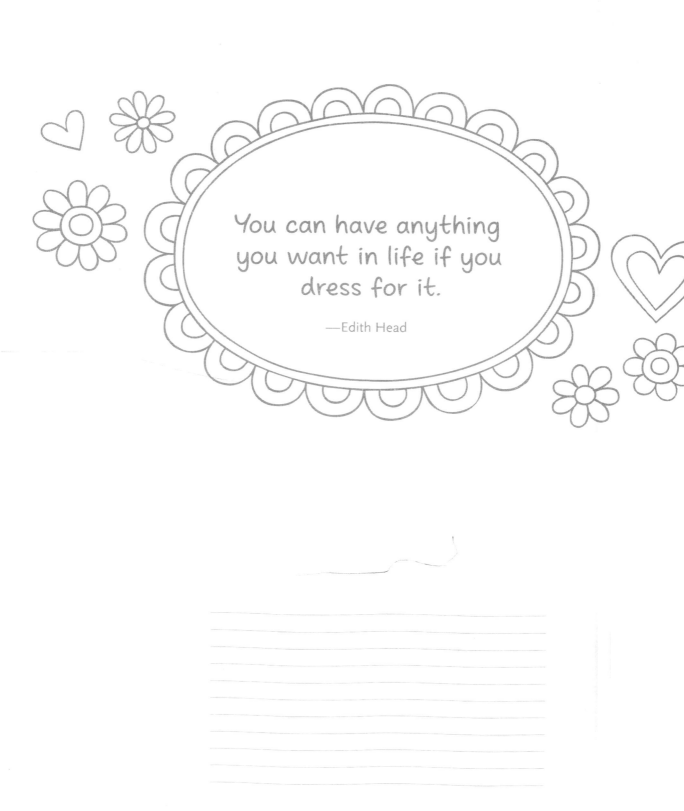

You can have anything you want in life if you dress for it.

—Edith Head

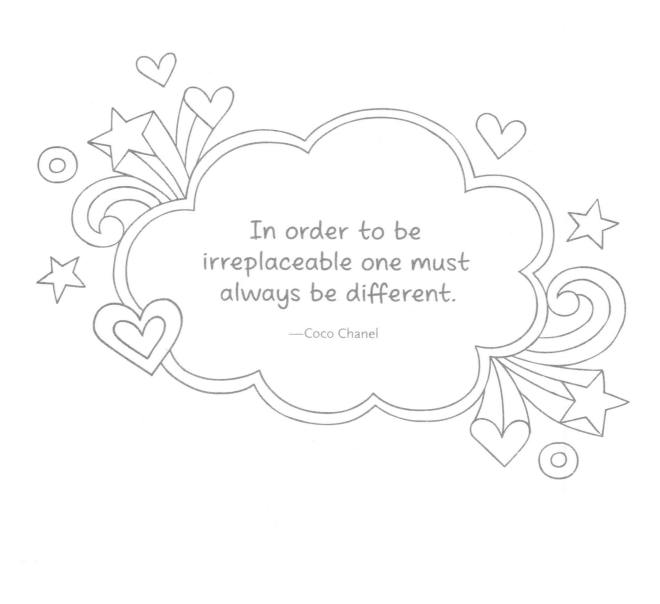

In order to be irreplaceable one must always be different.

—Coco Chanel

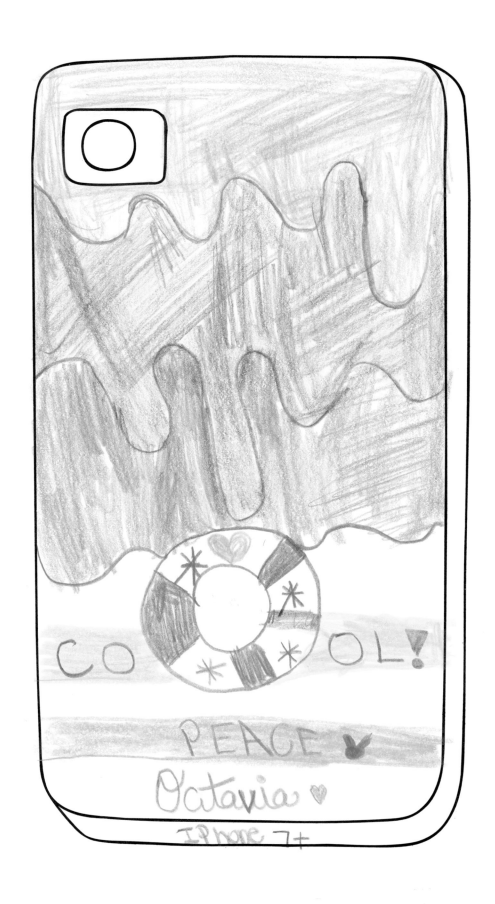

Now it's your turn to design your own fabulous phone case!

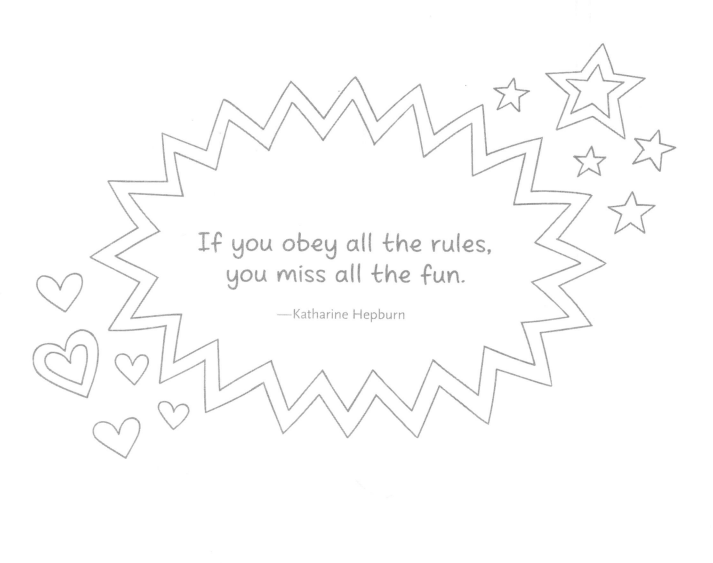

If you obey all the rules,
you miss all the fun.

—Katharine Hepburn

Add your own doodley details to these rainy-day fashions!

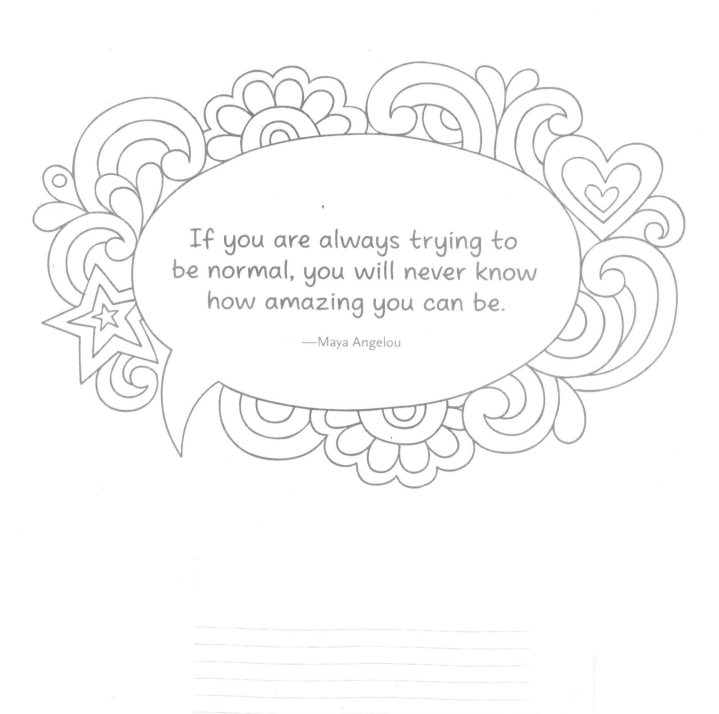

If you are always trying to be normal, you will never know how amazing you can be.

—Maya Angelou

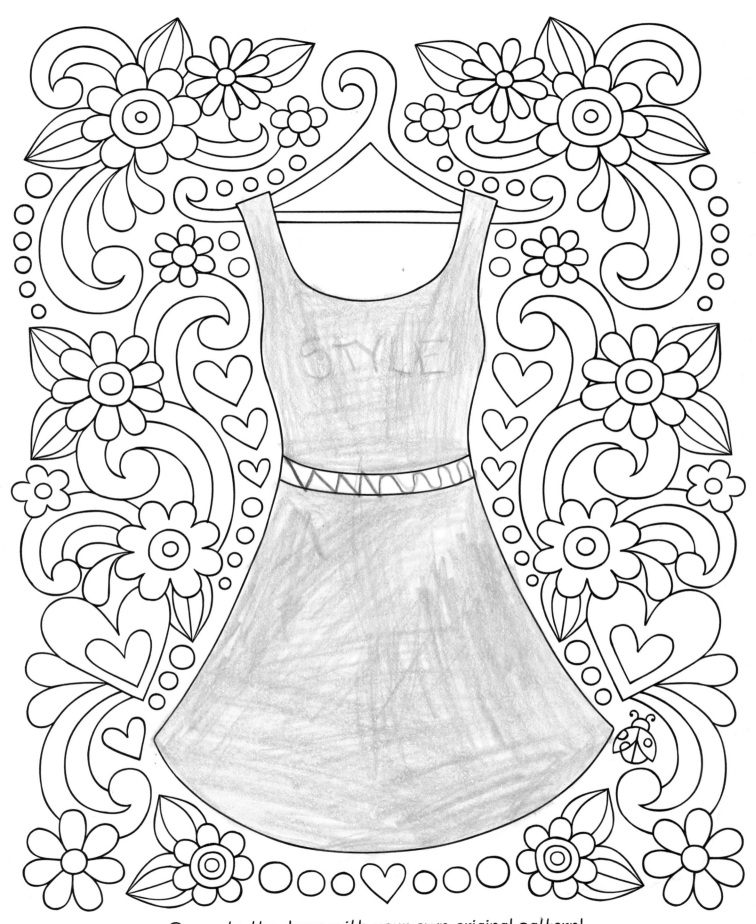

Decorate the dress with your own original pattern!

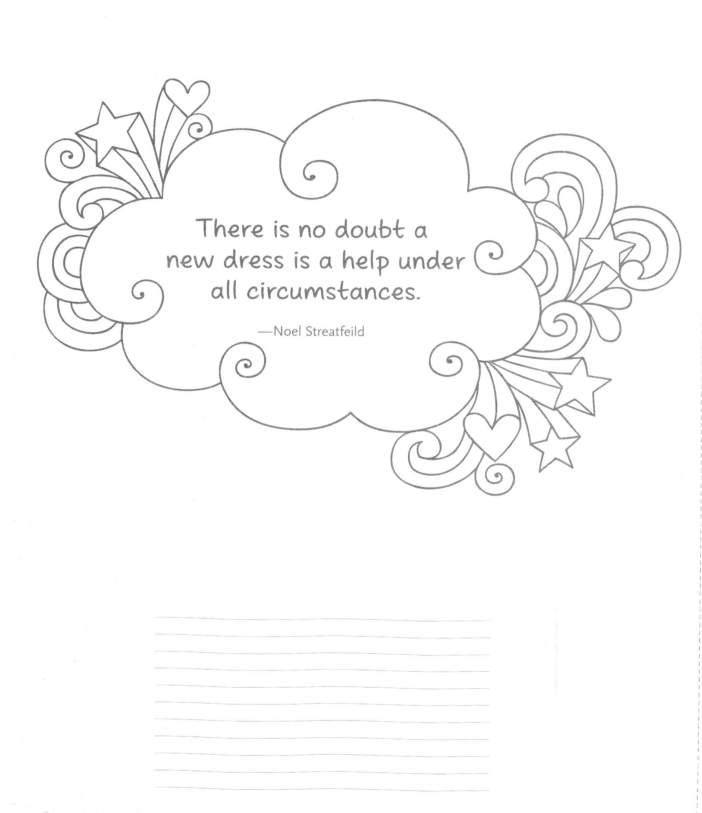

There is no doubt a
new dress is a help under
all circumstances.

—Noel Streatfeild

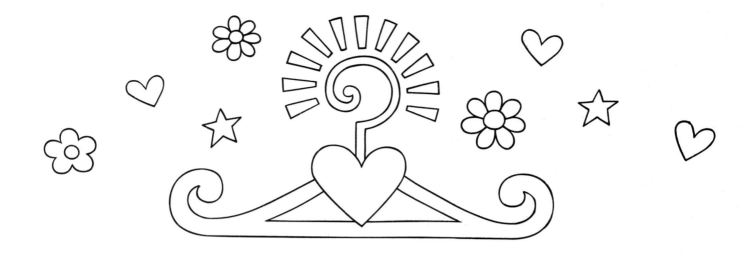

Now it's your turn! Design a dress that you would love to wear.

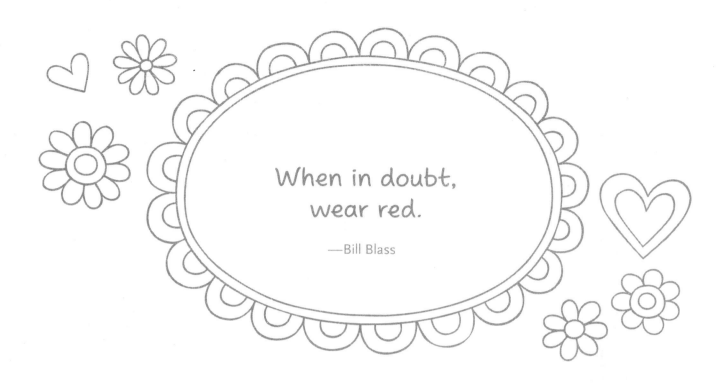

When in doubt,
wear red.

—Bill Blass

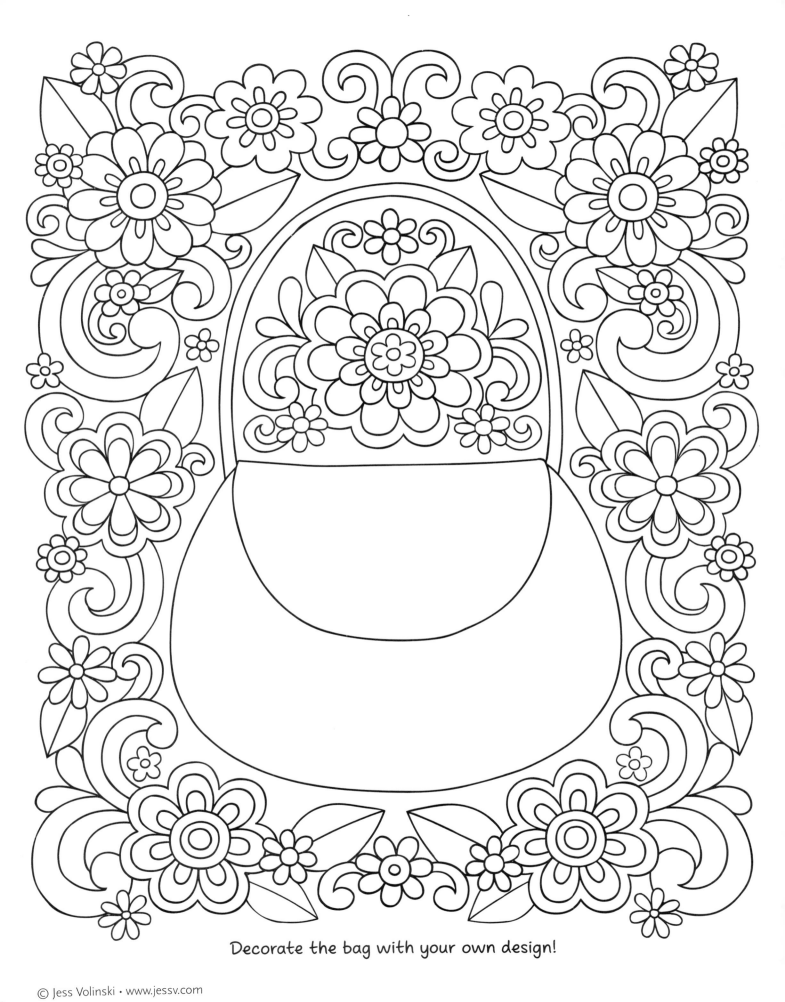

Decorate the bag with your own design!

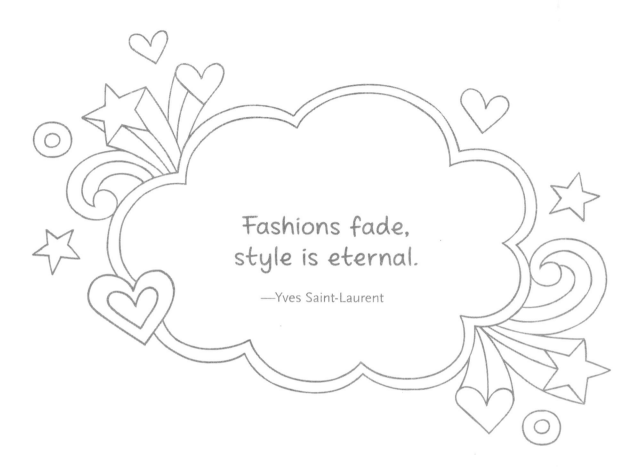

Fashions fade,
style is eternal.

—Yves Saint-Laurent

Doodle your favorite bag in the frame.

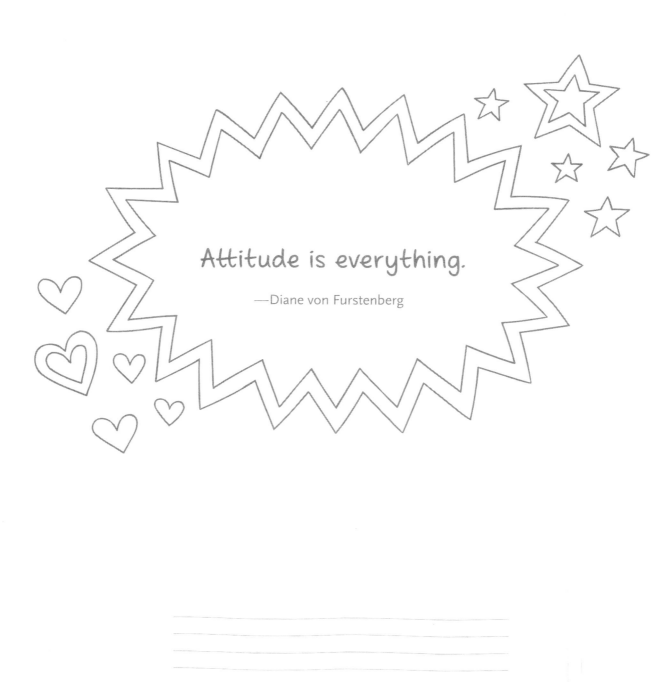

Attitude is everything.

—Diane von Furstenberg

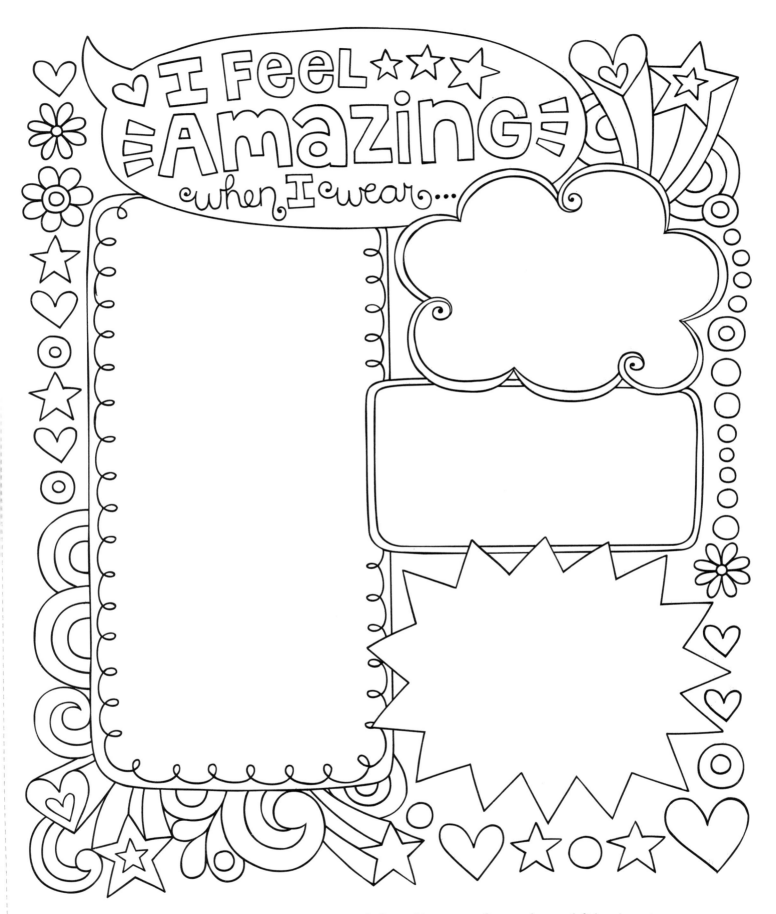

What clothes make you shine? Doodle your favorite outfit, shoes, and accessories in the bubbles!

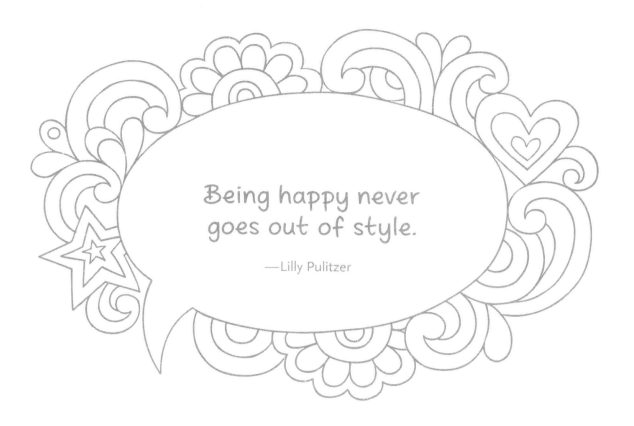

Being happy never
goes out of style.

—Lilly Pulitzer

What's in your bag?

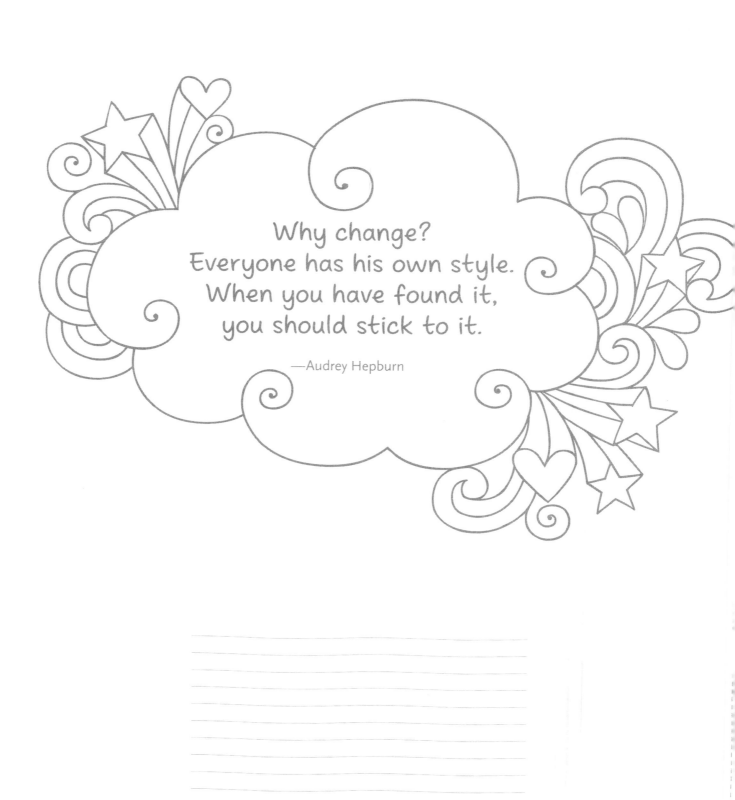

Why change?
Everyone has his own style.
When you have found it,
you should stick to it.

—Audrey Hepburn

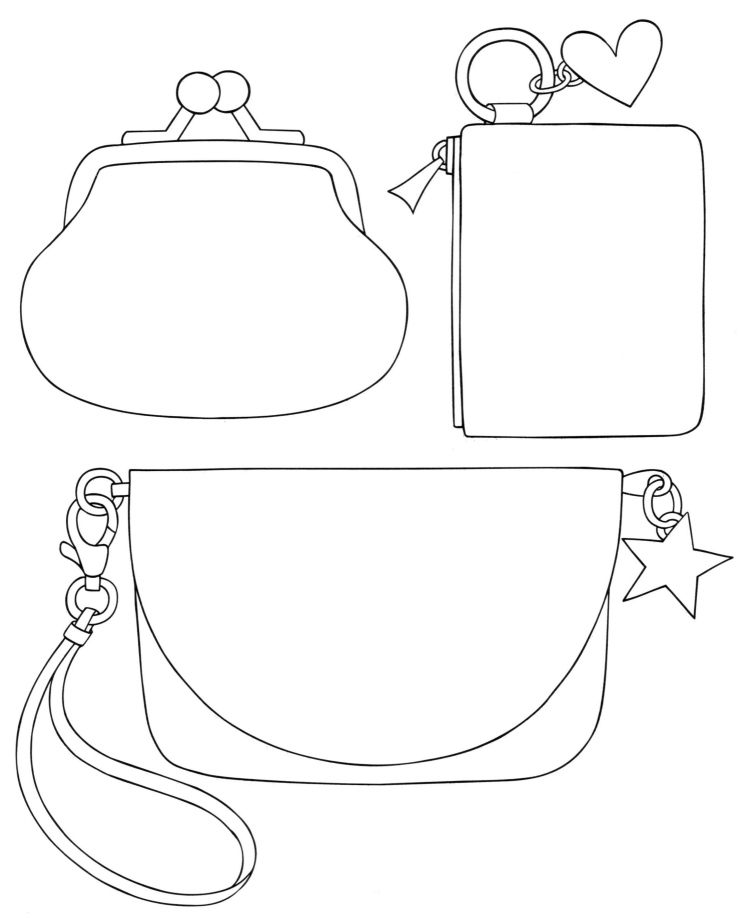

Decorate these cute purses with your own doodley designs!

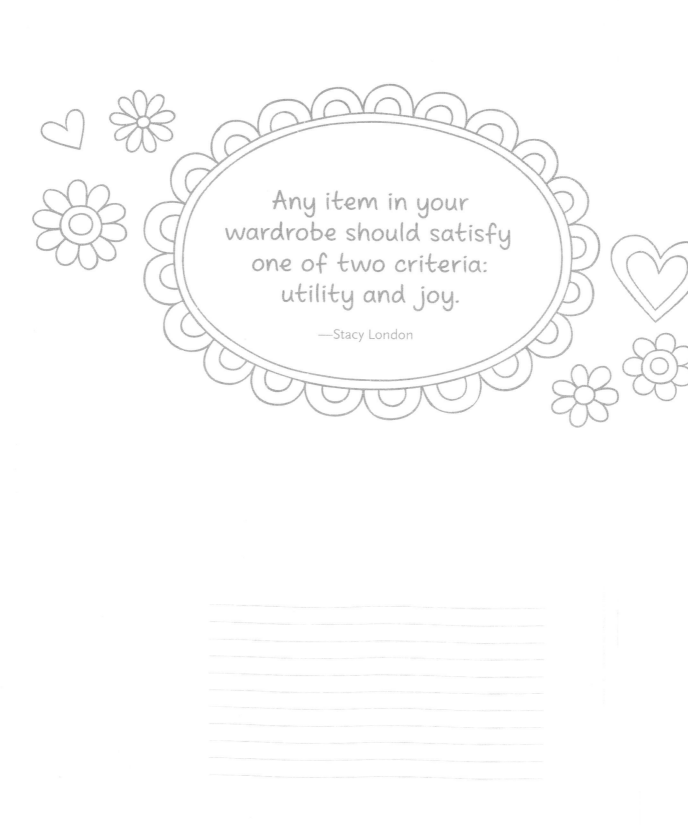

Any item in your wardrobe should satisfy one of two criteria: utility and joy.

—Stacy London

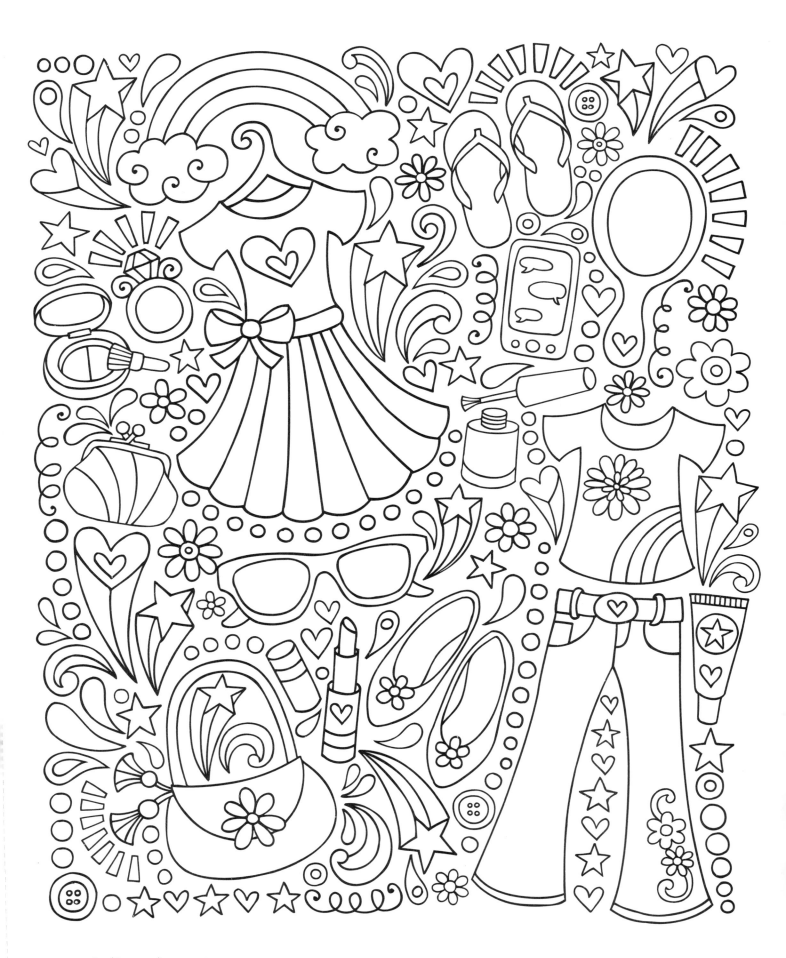

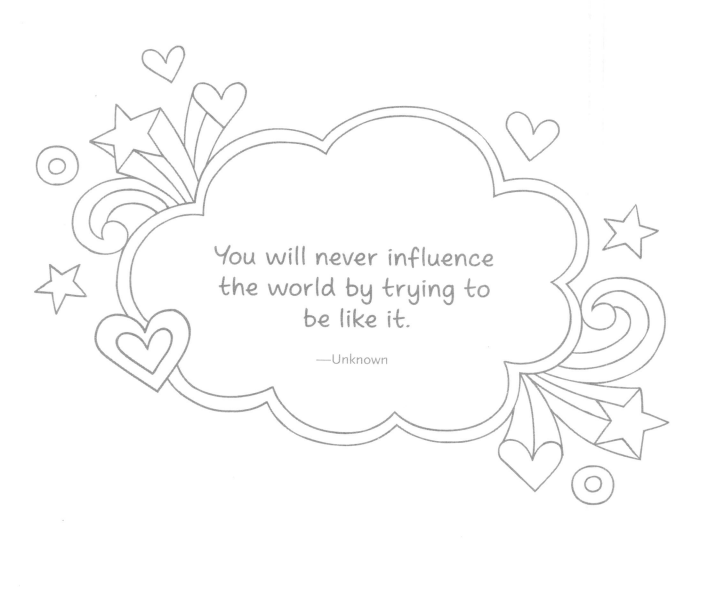

You will never influence the world by trying to be like it.

—Unknown

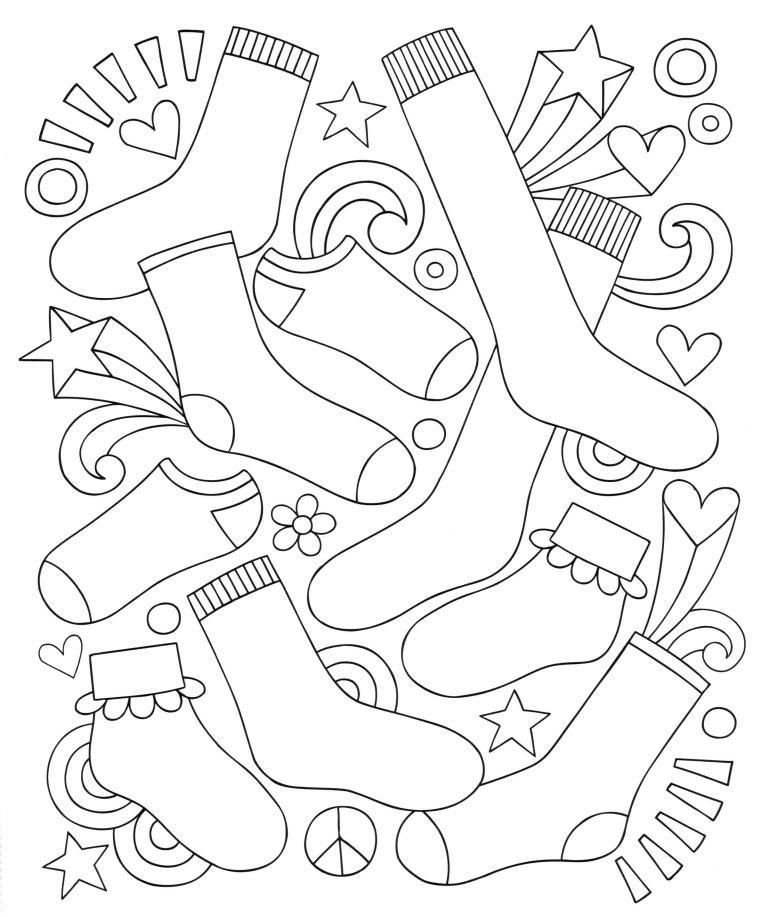

Add your own matching (or mismatching!) designs to the socks.

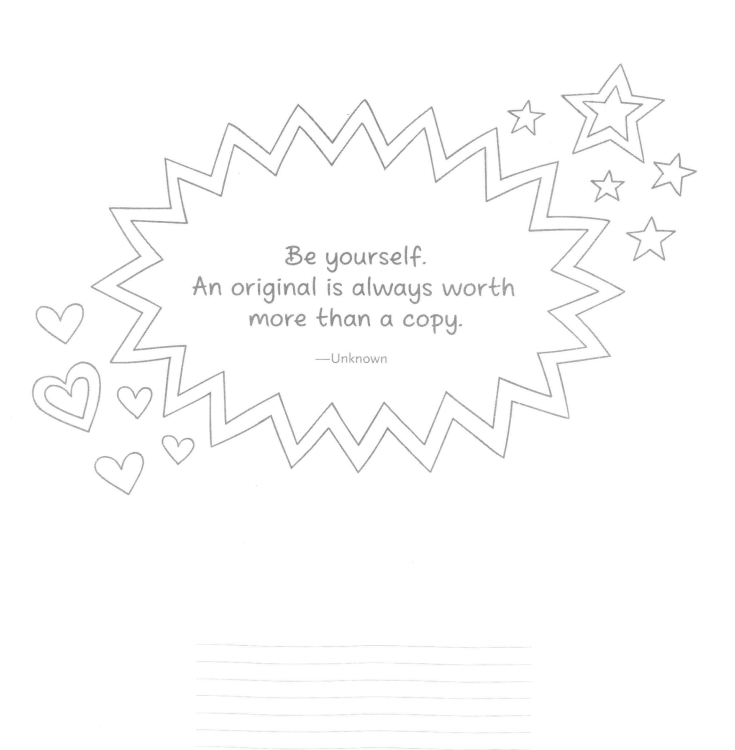

Be yourself.
An original is always worth
more than a copy.

—Unknown

_____
_____
_____
_____
_____
_____
_____

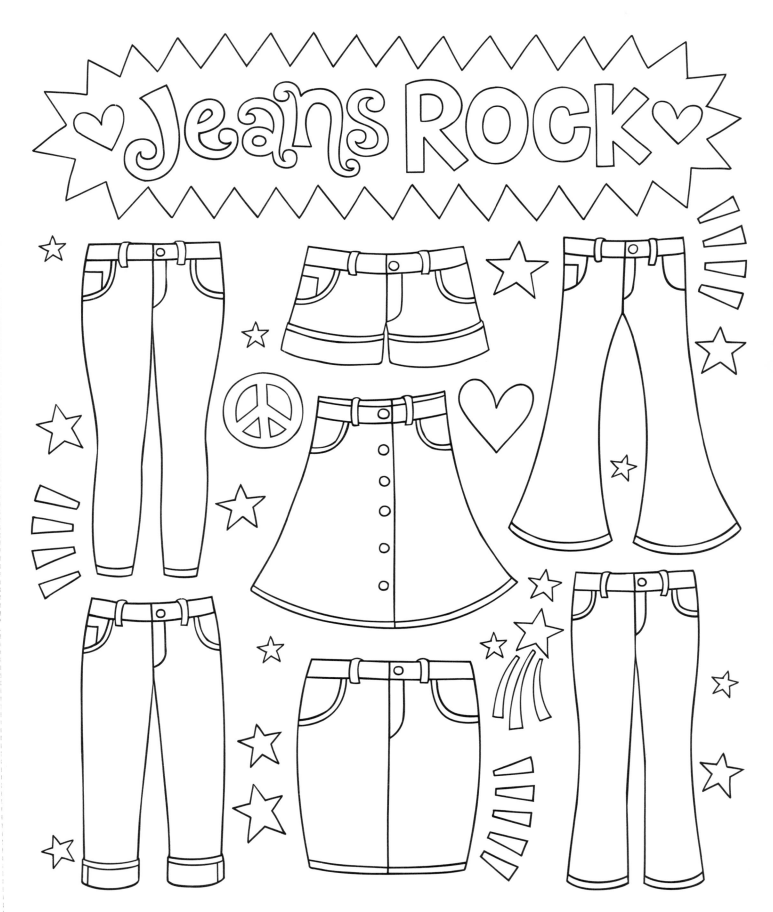

Customize the jeans with your own doodley embellishments!

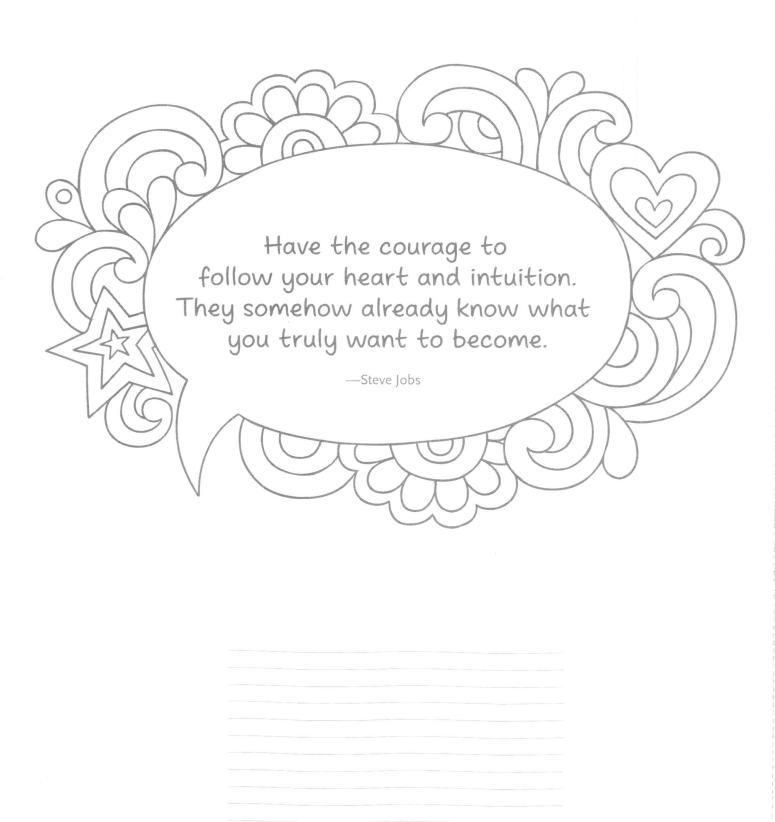

Have the courage to
follow your heart and intuition.
They somehow already know what
you truly want to become.

—Steve Jobs

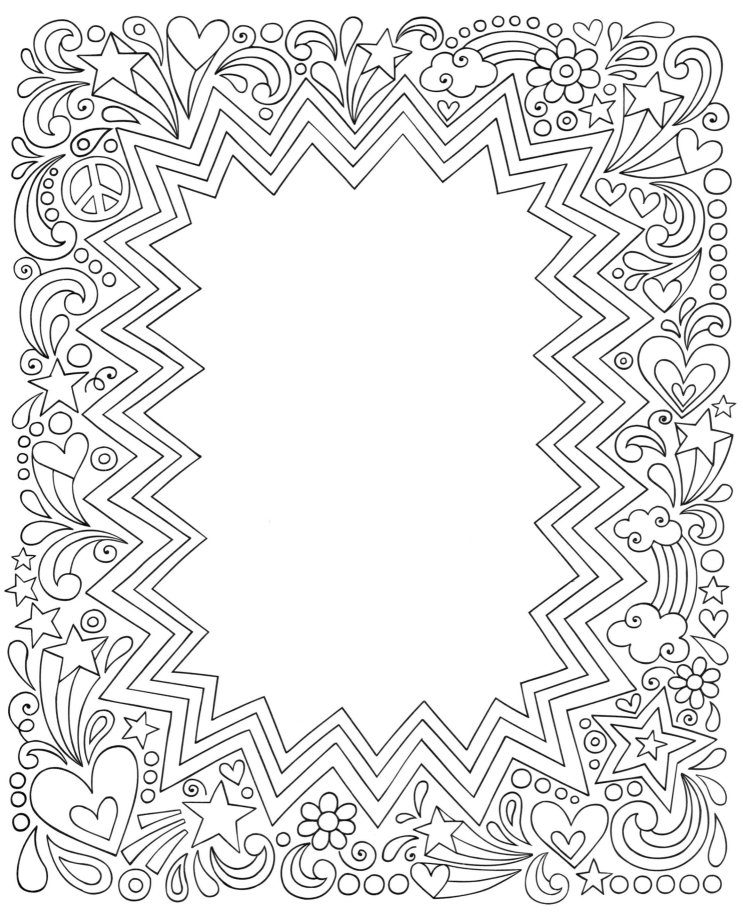

Now it's your turn! Doodle your favorite jeans in the frame.

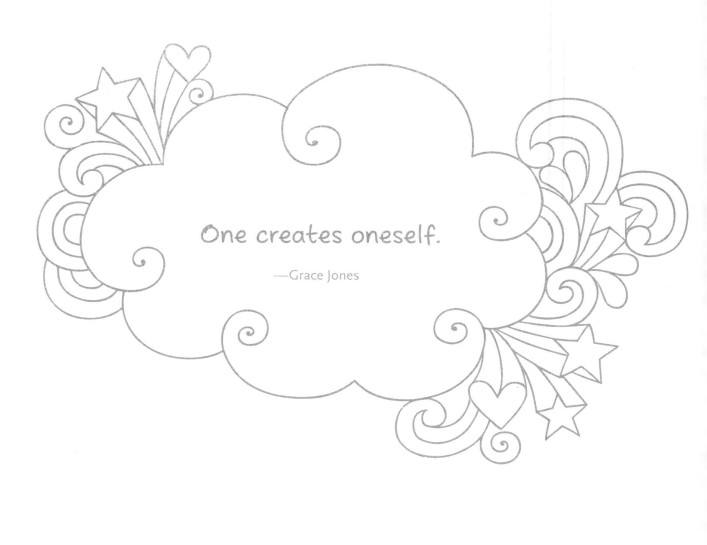

One creates oneself.

—Grace Jones

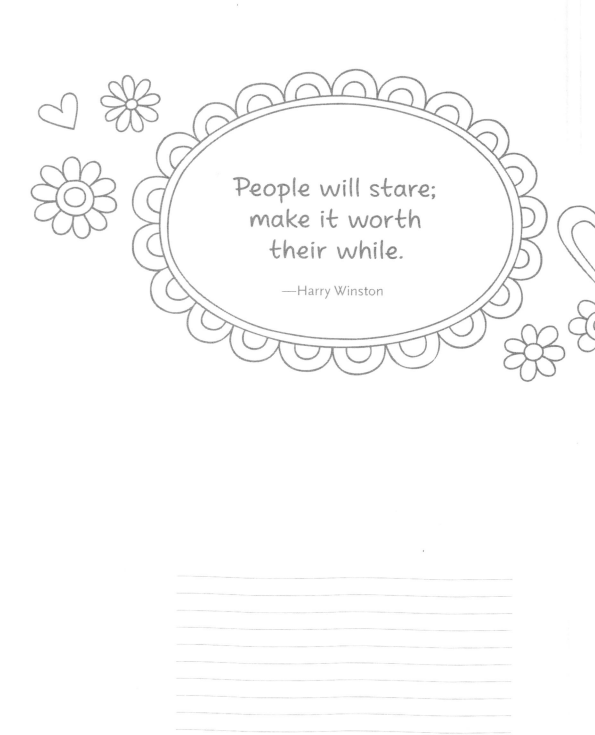

People will stare;
make it worth
their while.

—Harry Winston

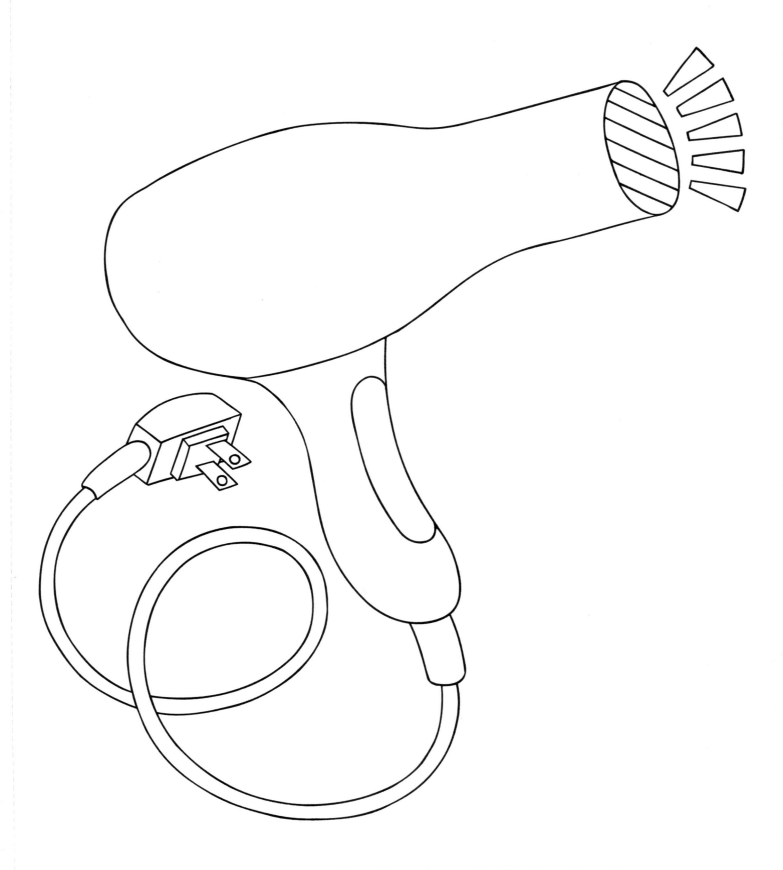

Add your own original surface design to the hair dryer!

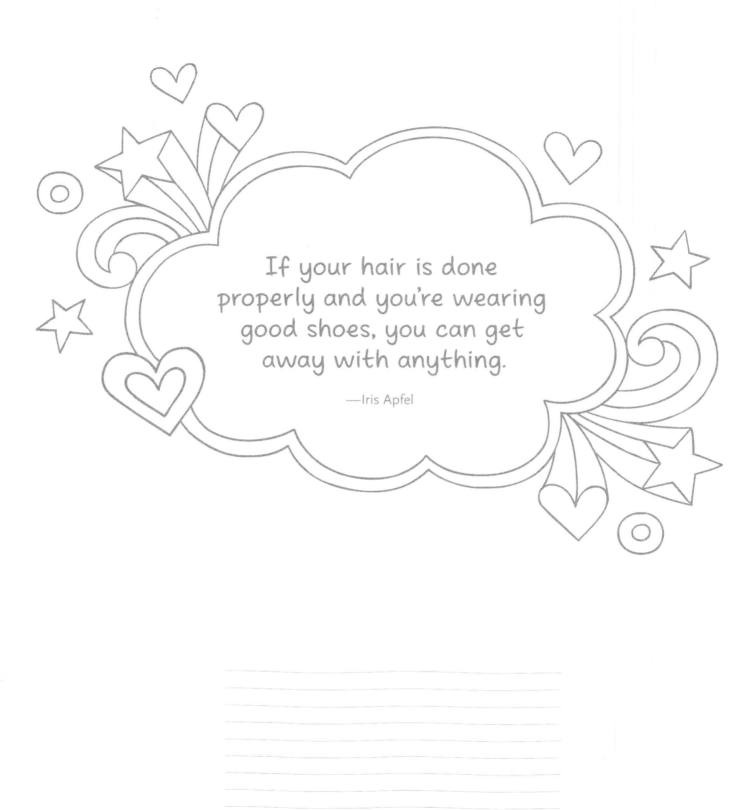

If your hair is done properly and you're wearing good shoes, you can get away with anything.

—Iris Apfel

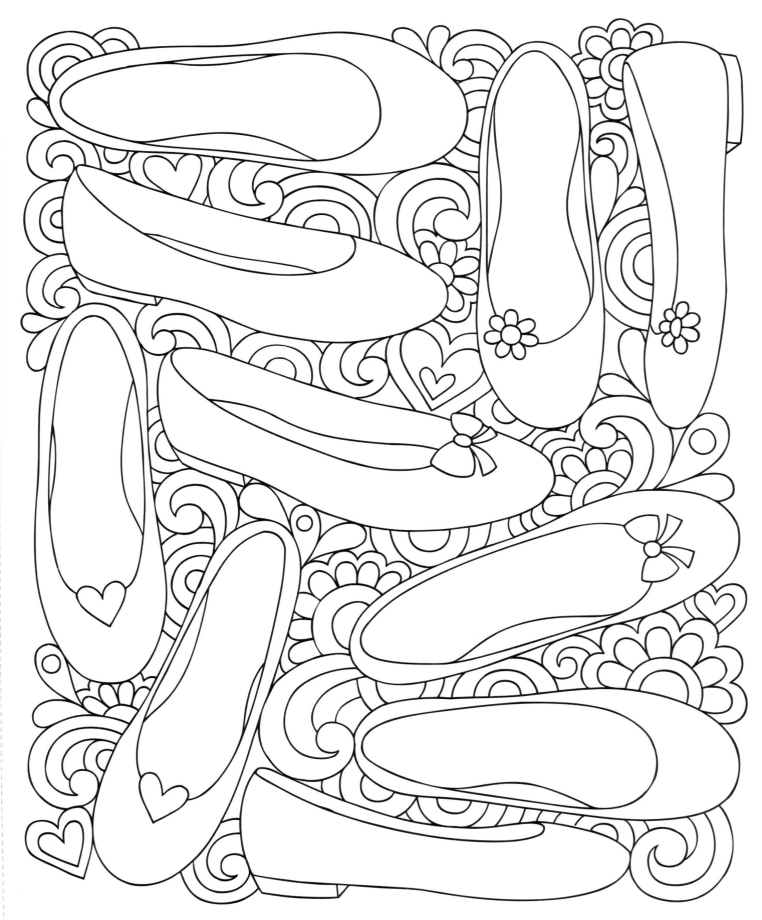

Doodle your own patterns on the ballet flats!

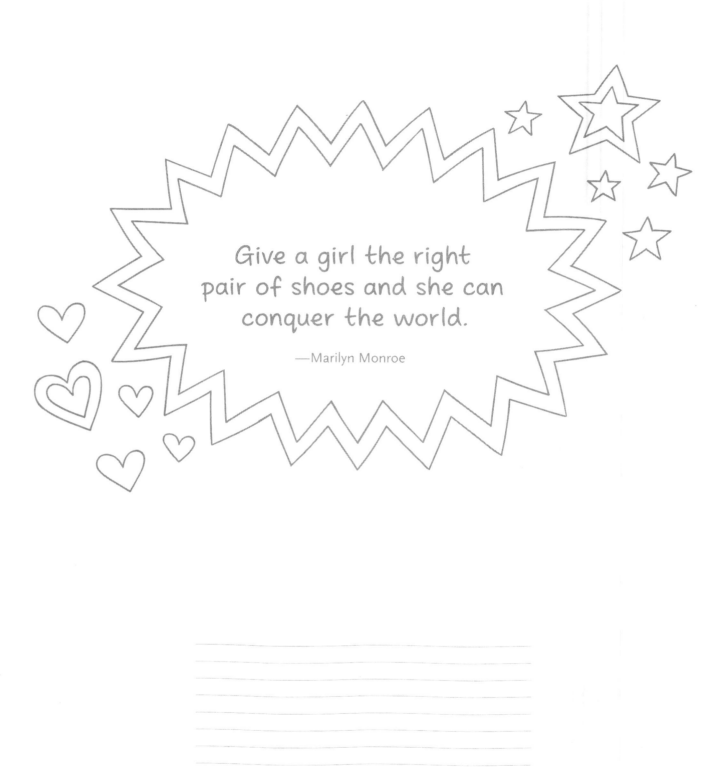

Give a girl the right
pair of shoes and she can
conquer the world.

—Marilyn Monroe

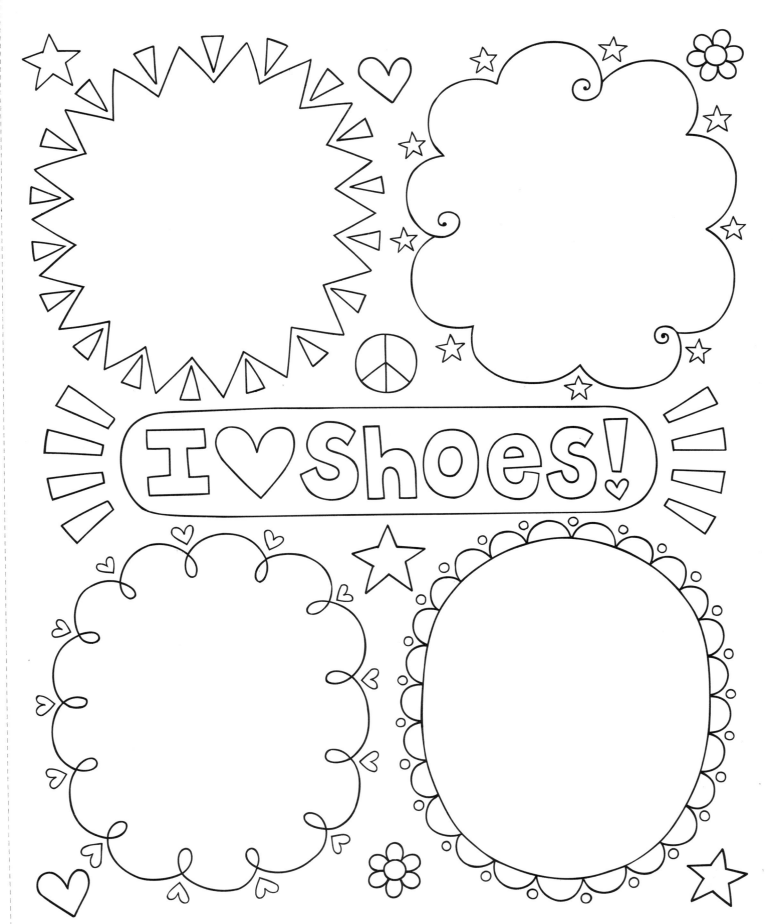

Now it's your turn! Doodle your favorite shoes from your closet
(or design your own amazing creations)!

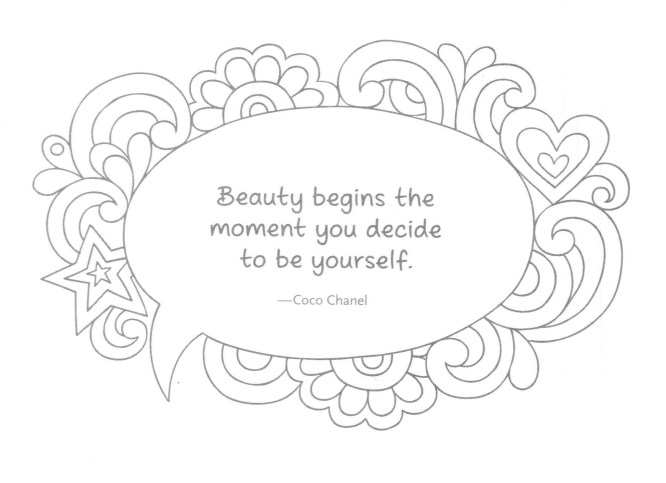

Beauty begins the moment you decide to be yourself.

—Coco Chanel

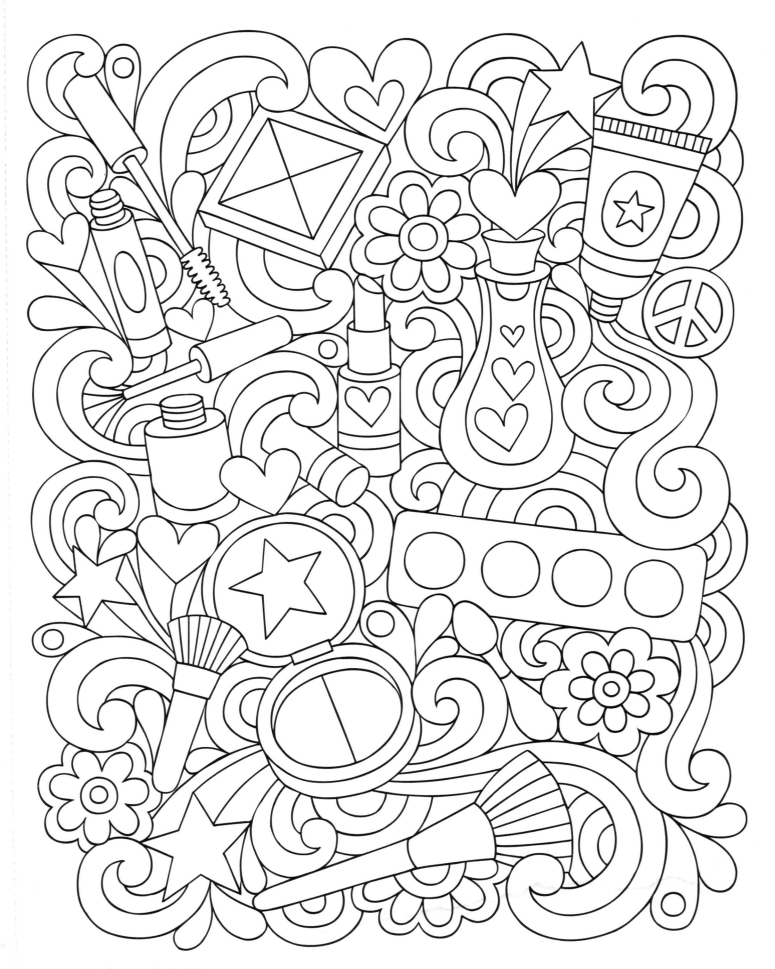

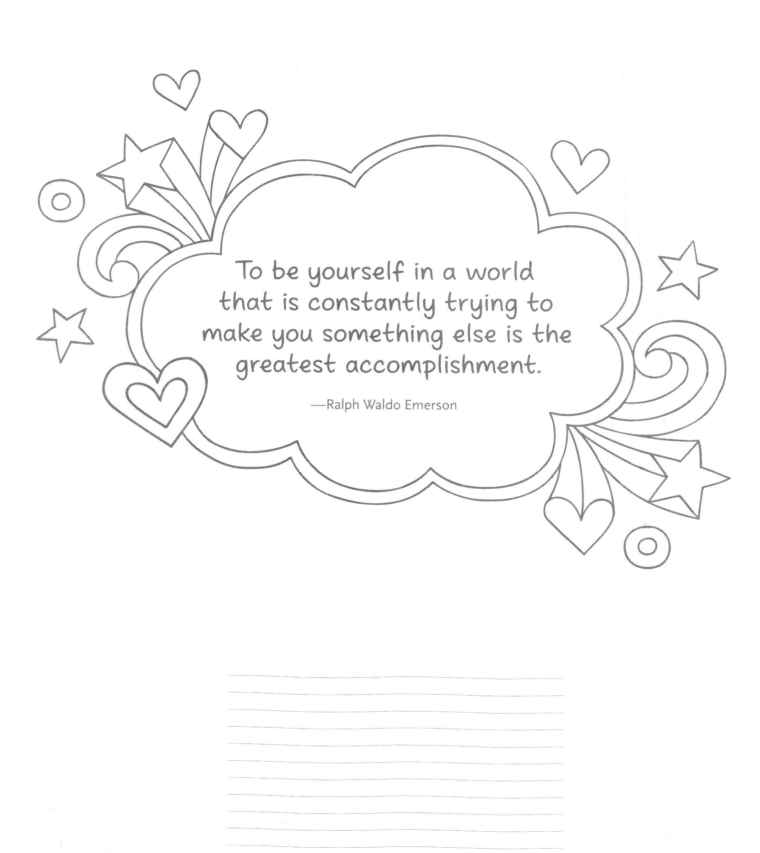

To be yourself in a world that is constantly trying to make you something else is the greatest accomplishment.

—Ralph Waldo Emerson

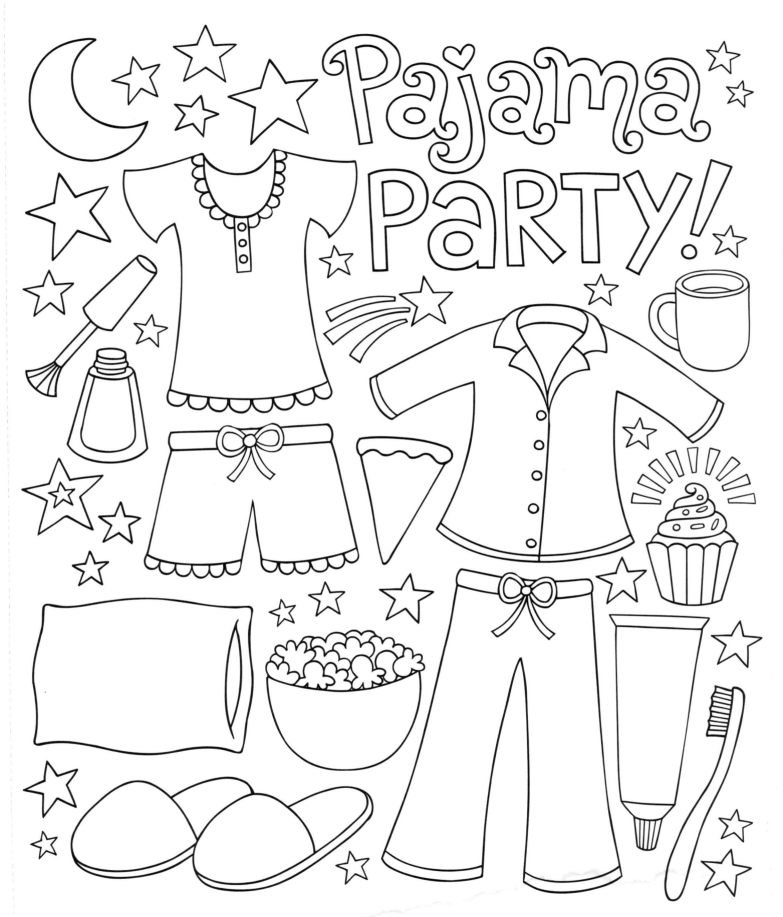

Party time! Doodle your own dreamy patterns on the pajamas, pillow, and slippers.

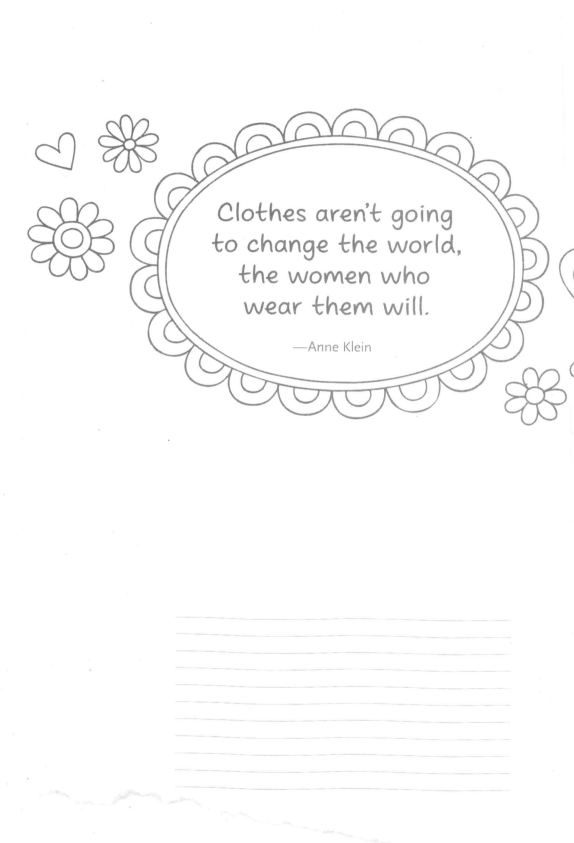

Clothes aren't going
to change the world,
the women who
wear them will.

—Anne Klein